Unshakable Resilience

*Build Unbreakable Strength, Will, and Hope
to Live Well in Times of Uncertainty*

By Zoe McKey

Copyright © 2020 by Zoe McKey. All rights reserved.

No part of this publication may be reproduced, stored in a retrieval system, or transmitted in any form or by any means, electronic, mechanical, photocopying, recording, scanning or otherwise, except as permitted under Section 107 or 108 of the 1976 United States Copyright Act, without the prior written permission of the author.

Limit of Liability/ Disclaimer of Warranty: The author makes no representations or warranties with respect to the accuracy or completeness of the contents of this work and specifically disclaims all warranties, including without limitation warranties of fitness for a particular purpose. No warranty may be created or extended by sales or promotional materials. The advice and recipes contained herein may not be suitable for everyone. This work is sold with the understanding that the author is not engaged in rendering medical, legal or other professional advice or services. If professional assistance is required, the services of a competent professional person should be sought. The author shall not be liable for damages arising herefrom. The fact that an individual, organization of website is referred to in this work as a citation and/or potential source of further information does not mean that the author endorses the information the individual, organization to website may provide or recommendations they/it may make. Further, readers should be aware that Internet websites listed in this work might have changed or disappeared between when this work was written and when it is read.

For general information on the products and services or to obtain technical support, please contact the author.

CREATED BY

ZOE MCKEY

SELF-DISCOVERY
~Starter Kit~

Thank you for choosing my book! I would like to show my appreciation for the trust you gave me by giving a **FREE GIFT** to you!

Visit www.zoemckey.com to get further information.

The kit shares *10 key practices to help you to:*
- *discover your true self,*
- *find your life areas that need improvement,*
- *find self-forgiveness,*
- *become better at socializing,*
- *lead a life of gratitude and purpose.*

The kit contains extra actionable worksheets with practice exercises for deeper learning.

Table of Contents

Table of Contents 9

Introduction 11

Chapter 1—Limited Space, Unlimited Time 15

Chapter 2—Take Care of Yourself 39

Chapter 3—How to Deal with Uncertainty 67

Chapter 4—How to Deal with Anxiety 93

Chapter 5—How to De-escalate Conflict at Home 149

In Closing… 163

Before you go… 167

Reference 179

Endnotes 183

Introduction

Know that you're not alone.

We're all in this together.

I am here for you, and I'm here to share some words of comfort, the best information, and some encouraging ideas to improve your life. I don't know you but I'm thinking about you, I am meditating for you, and I am sending you a lot of love, positive energy, and a virtual hand squeeze.

We'll be okay.

My intention is to support and serve you in these challenging times. In this book, I will share with you the best exercises, tips, and advice on how to get through these challenging times—together.

It's only day two in my self-chosen quarantine, but I have already managed to outline the premise of a new cult that we're about to launch from home with my friend.

It all started with him telling me he's about to brew his own kombucha. While planning where in the house we should set up a bonfire to enable the mass production of the fermented delicatessen, I subtly suggested that we should call ourselves a witch and a wiccan and sell our kombucha from our balcony, brand naming it Witch's Brew. We'd hire black cats, who'd ride brooms to satisfy long-distance delivery requests. My friend corrected me that wiccans are actually not male witches (as I thought) but different kinds of witches who follow the belief system of the Wicca. Or something like that. So not only did we manage to come up with a great and very feasible business idea on day two of our quarantine, we also dug deeper into witchcraft theory and history.

On day three of the quarantine, today, I decided that as much as I'd love to proceed with the plans of day two, I should really pursue goals that will help people in different ways. Like how to not go crazy and start a kombucha-brewing cult while in quarantine. Or how to not start a bonfire in your living room. Neither of these are recommended.

The world has turned into something unrecognizable. I can easily recall how I toasted with my two best friends on New Year's Eve for a brighter and better 2020. Today, one of them lost her job because the spa she was working at shut down indefinitely. The other one went from the chef of a prestigious restaurant to a butcher in a supermarket from one day to the other. And he's one of the lucky ones, still having a job.

We are all surrounded by uncertainty. This situation is so unfamiliar. And unfamiliarity gives birth to stress, fear, and anxiety. Some people experience a deep sense of hopelessness now. It is needed more than ever to hear uplifting words, share the best coping practices, and show a little care.

Chapter 1—Limited Space, Unlimited Time

We are facing challenges that we haven't before. Some people who were born in 1920 were unknowingly witnessing the devastation the Spanish flu caused. But people younger than a century haven't yet experienced a pandemic, which traveled over borders so quickly and required such strict prevention measures to slow the spread.

Our stress, fear, and anxiety levels are much higher now than, I dare say, a few weeks before. These emotions can become overwhelming and harmful, so learning to cope with them is crucial. While we all face the same stressor—COVID-19—the reactions we give to it may vary. Our response is partially influenced by our upbringing, our general stress tolerance, our support group's quality, and our willingness to be reasonable.

Other aspects that determine how we cope are age, health conditions, and risk to exposure. Older people, immunosuppressed people, people with lung problems, doctors, first responders, and people who have problems with substance usage might experience higher levels of stress than the general public.

People who are not at high risk can face extreme anxiety and fear as well—for the lives of their loved ones, for financial setbacks, or because of plans they had to postpone indefinitely. There is just so much going on right now.

Self-care, taking care of your family, friends, and community can help alleviate anxiety in you and those around you. Showing kindness towards yourself and other people is essential in the world we live today.

Why Should You Stay Home?

It's important to understand that the point of quarantine/social distancing/isolation is not to prevent us all from getting sick. The goal of the quarantine is to slow the spread of the virus and prevent overwhelming the healthcare system.

While many people get infected, about 10-15% of them need to be hospitalized. According to current data, epidemiologists predict that we can expect 40-70% of the world's population to be infected in the following year. That's a lot of people. But maybe, just for the argument's sake, the predictions are exaggerated and about 30% of the world's population gets infected instead. That's about 110 million people in the United States alone. This means that about 11-16 million will need a hospital bed in the next 12 months.

However, there are only roughly 925,000 hospital beds in the US, and a good two-thirds of those already have occupants: people who have cancer, a heart attack, regular maladies…

So, I can understand that from a 30-year-old's perspective, staying at home seems like a stretch and uncalled for. From a systems point of view, it's not only the smart but also the essential thing to do. The more people walk outside, the faster the virus will spread. The faster it spreads, the more hospital beds will be needed. The more beds get occupied, the harder choices doctors have to make—namely, who gets treated and who doesn't. Some people will not get the treatment they need and die unnecessarily.

It sounds harsh, but unfortunately, this is not a movie script. This is reality. So yes, you may not die from this disease. You may not even get very sick. But you can make others sick, and they can die. So, stay home. It's that simple.

What Is COVID-19 and How Do You Deal with It?

I know, all you read and hear about these days is about the coronavirus. I promise I will be short about the virus itself, but as a big advocate of lifelong learning and self-education, I find it my moral duty to equip you with accurate information on this global crisis. So much misguiding, false information is circulating out there about the virus that some people might find it hard to decide what to believe and what not.

The World Health Organization (WHO) and the Centers for Disease Control and Prevention (CDC) are two of the most reliable resources people can use to inform themselves. I heavily rely on these platforms where the world's leading experts are publishing their knowledge.

According to the CDC, these are the essentials that you need to know about COVID-19:

"Fact 1: Diseases can make anyone sick regardless of their race or ethnicity. Fear and anxiety about COVID-19 can cause people to avoid or reject others even though they are not at risk for spreading the virus."[i]

I have a beloved friend. She is an American-born Chinese girl and a new mom. A few days ago we had a conversation where she confessed that she's not as afraid of the virus as she is of racism, violence, and hostility directed towards people of Asian descent. It breaks my heart to know that she lives in fear because she's Chinese even though she's never been to China and heard about Wuhan for the first time when I did.

This is the time where humanity needs to come together as one, not to separate. Collective punishment and racist comments won't make the virus go away. Our goal is to protect people who are vulnerable, make sure to get rid of this virus, and go back to our lives as we know it. So let's focus on what helps us get there. Here are some more facts and protection advice from the CDC:

"Fact 2: For most people, the immediate risk of becoming seriously ill from the virus that causes COVID-19 is thought to be low.

Older adults and people of any age with underlying health conditions, such as diabetes, lung disease, or heart disease, are at greater risk of severe illness from COVID-19.

Fact 3: Someone who has completed quarantine or has been released from isolation does not pose a risk of infection to other people.

Fact 4: There are simple things you can do to help keep yourself and others healthy.

- Wash your hands often with soap and water for at least 20 seconds, especially after blowing your nose, coughing, or

sneezing; going to the bathroom; and before eating or preparing food.
- Avoid touching your eyes, nose, and mouth with unwashed hands.
- Stay home when you are sick.
- Cover your cough or sneeze with a tissue, then throw the tissue in the trash.

Fact 5: You can help stop COVID-19 by knowing the signs and symptoms:

- Fever
- Cough
- Shortness of breath

Seek medical advice if you

- Develop symptoms

AND

- Have been in close contact with a person known to have COVID-19 or live in or have recently traveled from an area with ongoing spread of COVID-19. Call ahead before you go to a doctor's office or emergency room. Tell them about your recent travel and your symptoms."[ii]

And here is a short list of what you shouldn't do:

1. You shouldn't leave your house without a homemade mask. News about masks have been generally contradictory in the past months. People were actively discouraged to buy up masks, stating that only those who are either COVID-19 symptomatic and need to go outside, or are taking care of someone who is COVID-19 symptomatic, should wear masks. The latest research proves that wearing masks, regardless of one's health condition, when we go outside to do our essential shopping

is actually helpful. It has been proven that there's no need to breathe in a giant sneeze to be exposed to the virus. Even while talking, small droplets can leave our mouth, and thus we can infect others or get infected ourselves.

However, even in light of this new information, we don't need the N95 masks. We should leave those to health care workers, who are experiencing a major shortage of them. What we should do instead is a DIY face mask project.

And hey, you can't have the excuse that you haven't got time.

The CDC released an article where they show a step-by-step tutorial on how to create your own mask within minutes. Check out this article to inform yourself of the latest mask-related advice: https://www.cdc.gov/coronavirus/2019-ncov/prevent-getting-sick/diy-cloth-face-coverings.html

2. Can someone explain to me what the deal is with the toilet paper hoarding? Seriously. I can understand a lot of things. If people would hoard Nutella, oatmeal, raspberries, or kittens, I get it. But toilet paper? There is an international shortage of toilet paper in stores. I spoke to friends in London, Manila, Budapest, and Cape Town and they all said the same thing, "There's no toilet paper in stores." This virus doesn't have diarrhea as its main symptom, people, you don't need to fill your garage with toilet paper and sit on top of it with a rifle to protect it.

If you are in the same shoes I am and can't buy even one scroll of toilet paper in stores, here are some alternatives: baby wipes; if you have it, a bidet; or the good ol' shower.

Jokes aside, being mindful about other people also includes being mindful of their needs. There is enough of everything for all of us as long as we all take just as much as we actually need. I know, these times are unknown and terrifying and we don't know how long this situation is going to last. However, so far supply chains are working, and as long as we mindfully consume, everyone will have their needs met. I'm not talking about toilet paper only, but bread, meat, milk, and other essentials.

I want to close this educational section with a funny thought; a comparison, rather, which will help you understand how to wash your hands. Wash your hands as if you wanted to insert contact lenses after chopping jalapeno peppers. Thoroughly.

By the way, on education...

Lead by Example as a Parent

Children, for better or for worse, mimic what they see their parents do. If a parent is freaking out, constantly worrying and complaining, the child will be exposed to a much higher risk of overstressing. Being well-prepared and well-informed is the first step in good crisis management. A stable base of knowledge and good problem-solving skills give a sense of confidence and calm.

Even if you do your best to stay calm and collected, your child might exhibit behavior that they outgrew, like bedwetting. Children are very susceptible to uncertainty so they may be more irritable, worried, and have a weaker attention span than before. If something like this happens, it is important to assure the child that they have nothing to feel ashamed of, that this is a normal reaction of the body to stress.

The CDC recommends parents talk to their children about the current pandemic, explain to them what's true about it and what's not, and reassure their kids of their safety. It's much better to validate the youngsters' emotions instead of pressuring them to repress what they feel. It's okay to be scared, it's okay to be anxious. As a role model, tell your children how you deal with stress.

Try to minimize your children's (and your own) exposure to unreliable or fearmongering resources such as social media platforms, sensationalist news channels, and other resources without credentials.

Maintaining a routine in the chaos is also important. Make sure to separate some time for self-care, for education, for fun, and for relaxation.[iii]

What Is Social Distancing?

Last year all I could hear was "get off your phone, go out and socialize." Now the new rage is "socialize on your phone and stay inside." How interesting that both of these recommendations can be sound if put in the right context!

Social distancing, quarantine, and isolation are concepts we hear fairly often these days. While we roughly know what they mean, it can be hard to explicitly tell the difference between them. I used the help of the Substance Abuse and Mental Health Services Administration (SAMHSA) to define each of them:

"Social distancing is a way to keep people from interacting closely or frequently enough to spread an infectious disease. Schools and other gathering places such as movie theaters may close, and sports events and religious services may be cancelled.

Quarantine separates and restricts the movement of people who have been exposed to a contagious disease to see if they become sick. It lasts long enough to ensure the person has not contracted an infectious disease.

Isolation prevents the spread of an infectious disease by separating people who are sick from those who are not. It lasts as long as the disease is contagious."[iv]

Our government has the right to enforce by law any of the three states mentioned above if they find it necessary to maintain the health and safety of the population. We don't have much influence over their decision. Being in quarantine, isolated, or practicing social distancing takes a toll on our emotions.

Many of us experience a given amount of worry, fear, and anxiety—for our loved ones and ourselves. But there are other emotions that we need to consider. For example, the anger, resentment, or confusion your friends and family members may feel if they have to enter in quarantine because of us. Or vice versa—we need to enter into quarantine because we had contact with a friend of ours who tested positive for the virus.

It can provoke negative feelings if strangers or loved ones are monitoring us for symptoms. My boyfriend is a doctor, and therefore his health is very important for the simple reason he can help sick people. If he is healthy, his skills are a help multiplier. If he is sick, many people won't get to see a doctor as fast, and some of his colleagues would have to cover his shifts. A few days ago he told me that if I show symptoms of COVID-19 he needs to first test for the illness, and if not, we need to stay separated for fourteen days for safety reasons. World-health goals beat our couple goals. I respect him for his mental fortitude and he is absolutely right. However, I'd be lying if I said I was overflowing with joy when I heard his words.

A classic fear trigger is potential or actual loss of income due to the closure of all nonessential businesses. In a later chapter I will talk extensively about dealing with the fear of financial loss.

Another catalyst for negative emotions is the actual or potential lacking of essential food and sanitation supplies.

We can feel a string of negative emotions for not being able to properly care for our loved ones; feeling frustrated and angry for needing to cancel future plans like holidays, weddings, birthdays, and anniversaries. We can feel lonely while being distanced from friends, family, social support groups, and activities we enjoy doing. We may feel bored and frustrated with being cut off from our normal life. We may want to use substances to cope with the current situation. Anger can be triggered when we see others being negligent about sanitation. I'm sure there are lots of demons arising in our solitude. It is certainly a difficult time, but we're in this together; as humanity, we're not alone—even if we are physically apart.

Stay <u>Moderately</u> Tuned in for <u>Accurate</u> Information

Our sense and perception of risk and danger can be skewed at times like this. Let's take a look at some of the most recent statistical data:

As of April 15th, there are 2,044,221 confirmed cases and 131,301 deaths recorded worldwide.[v]

Let's take a look at the COVID-19 fatality rate by age chart. Death Rate stands for the number of deaths / number of cases. Or in other words, the probability of dying if infected by the virus. This probability percentage differs depending on the age group. The percentages you see in the chart do not have to add up to 100%, as they don't represent share of deaths by age group. Rather, they show the risk of dying if infected with COVID-19 for someone in a given age group.[vi]

AGE	DEATH RATE confirmed cases	DEATH RATE all cases
80+ years old	21.9%	14.8%
70-79 years old		8.0%
60-69 years old		3.6%
50-59 years old		1.3%
40-49 years old		0.4%
30-39 years old		0.2%
20-29 years old		0.2%
10-19 years old		0.2%
0-9 years old		no fatalities

Picture 1: COVID-19 Fatality Rate by Age[vii]

As you can see, the fatality rate up to the age of 50 is lower and it gradually works itself up to close to 15 percent in the age group of 80+.

There is a difference between how the virus affects different genders. Statistically, males are more likely to die from the virus than females.

This difference can partially be attributed to the male-dominant smoking culture in China. Smoking increases the chance of developing respiratory problems. Here, just like in the other chart, death rate means the number of deaths divided by the number of cases, so the probability of dying if infected by the virus in terms of percentages.

SEX	DEATH RATE confirmed cases	DEATH RATE all cases
Male	4.7%	2.8%
Female	2.8%	1.7%

Picture 2: COVID-19 Death Rate by Gender[viii]

Enough charts for now. But if you must, follow the daily updates of www.wordometers.info. While it is our duty to stay informed about what's happening in the world—again, from reliable sources—obsessing about the news all day won't help us. Our level of anxiety can grow proportionally with the consumption of COVID-19 news.

Watch *Downton Abbey* instead. I just restarted watching this show; it's still perfect.

Chapter 2—Take Care of Yourself

Meet Your Basic Needs

Tony Robbins is America's leading life and business strategist. I have listened to his coaching sessions and videos for years. As a returning listener of his, I bump into the same information he shares from time to time. As I sat and thought about what to write in this book to help you as much as possible, I recalled Robbins' words about the six basic human needs. One of them is the need for certainty, which today sounds more needed than ever. He argues that one of these needs is usually more dominant for us than the other five, and that this dominance varies from person to person.

Let's take a look at our six human needs and what we can do to satisfy each of them as much as we can.

The Need for Certainty

The need for stability and predictability is a core human need. Those people who look for certainty in life are generally seeking safety, security, and predictability about the future. What scares us or makes us feel anxiety is not the event of a bad experience—rather, when we're not sure whether a bad experience will happen or not. When something bad happens, at least we know about it; we can take ownership of it, we can be certain of what it is, we can control it, and we have the power and opportunity to fix it. But when our life becomes unpredictable we feel as though we've lost control.

The pitfall of the need for strong certainty is that nothing in life is truly certain—only taxes and death. So when some aspire to feel safe about their environment, they might become over-controlling, irrational, or perfectionistic. They avoid pain and seek pleasure more than usual, all for catering to a fragile sense of certainty.

I am definitely one of these people. I like when my life is predictable and when it feels safe. But as many events before—and this pandemic now—prove, having a certain sense of certainty is wishful thinking at best and delusional at worst. Things will certainly change—just like the seasons, our age, everything around us.

It's not a bad thing to aim for creating as much certainty as possible in our lives, but the key is to not get too attached to it. Stay flexible. Do the best you can every time, do research. We should try our best to choose the best house to buy, the best stocks to invest in, the best school for our children, the best career path for ourselves, the best partner to share our life with; it's good to try to make the best, safest choices in all these areas... and then be prepared to be wrong. Or for the world to go off track. Like now.

What's the best we can do right now? I'm not planning to give a definite answer to this question because I'm asking it constantly, day in and day out. What seems the best to do today might not be the best choice tomorrow. I may need to start every day with this question. What's the best I can do today? And then do just that.

This is a period of uncertainty, of transition. The best we, the certainty seekers, can do right now is to find certainty one day at a time and be ready to shift, change, morph, and adapt to whatever tomorrow brings.

The Need for Uncertainty

Oh boy, those people who have uncertainty as their top need must be thriving right now. These guys love changes. They enjoy variety, risks (even the unnecessary ones); they live and die for a good hit of adrenaline... All the explorers, extreme sport junkies, stock market addicts, gamblers, raise your hands.

The good news is, we live in a time when your gutsy way of being you can cash in big amounts of money, success, and fame because you dare wander to places most wouldn't. The bad news is, you can also lose everything, because such is the nature of uncertainty.

While times like these are meant for you to blossom, I'd like to gently caution you to evaluate risk-reward scenarios before you go, "Dang it, I'll put all my money in the stock market because now is the time."

These people are the Elon Musks and Thomas Edisons of the world. But they are also the Steve

Irwins and Ayrton Sennas, who weren't so lucky while pushing the limits of uncertainty.

The Need for Significance

Do you care a lot about people's opinion of you? Do you love to be heard, seen, admired, recognized for your efforts—a bit more than the general public? If so, this may be your top need. You love to stand out in the crowd, to feel special—and be made feeling special. You find validation in such feedback.

Significance today can be "measured" by social media. The more likes (or shares, or views) we get, the more significant we feel. And vice versa.

Significance has been an extremely important human need ever since our ancestors came out of the caves. If others find us an important part of the community, it boosts our chances for survival. Recognition for our efforts can make us more productive, which attracts even more recognition and puts us on a positive reinforcing feedback loop.

The negative side of wanting to feel significant is when people engage in unhealthy behavior to get it. Abusing certain substances to get a feeling of a high, being argumentative (becoming that one family member everybody is tiptoeing around), and surrounding oneself with less skilled people to appear superior are just a few tactics some might use to feel more important.

Being in quarantine makes it hard to get face-to-face recognition from people. Luckily, we can use the power of the internet for something good—spreading love, peace, and supportive messages around, which many people will value and appreciate. We can be a significant pillar in our community; holding the hands of those who need it the most virtually.

The Need for Love

We are social beings wired for seeking love and connection. To some people the fulfillment of this need is at the center of their lives. They wish to have close relationships, to belong. Their loyalty and love is a gift to others. But in extreme cases they care so much about others that they have little room left for self-care. We know that in order to love someone, well, first we need to love ourselves. In order to care for someone we need to know how to take care of ourselves.

This has never been more true than today. We need to stay healthy—mentally, physically, and spiritually—to be able to be the pillar for our loved ones. Make sure that you take proper care of your health. Get daily exercise even if there's nowhere to do it but your own living room. Drink some tea. Meditate. Do yoga. Watch an uplifting movie. You're reading an uplifting book, good job for doing this for yourself!

The Need for Growth

"In this world you're either growing or you're dying, so get in motion and grow." — Lou Holtz

Those who value growth the most as a basic need are always trying to improve and learn. Usually they are very good at what they do; they work hard to master their vocation. They also have a tendency to move on when they feel they've reached their full potential or as though they can't learn anything anymore. The upside of being growth oriented is always being in motion, not getting bored. The downside of it can be burnout, ignorance of our physical and mental limits, and turning a blind eye to declining health or high stress levels.

While being isolated leaves a lot of time and energy to learn and grow, we need to do it in moderation. We need to be kind to ourselves, and give our mind and body a break when we feel we need it. There's no rush, we have nowhere to be. Some of the best growth opportunities take root in the silence.

The Need for Contribution

"The secret to living is giving." — Tony Robbins

You like people and you feel happy when people are happy. Making a difference in your community or on a bigger scale therefore is important to you. While giving to others selflessly is noble, don't forget that giving should start at home to those closest to you. So many times we take our loved ones for granted while being extremely present and devoted to strangers. If you hear your spouse or children complaining "you're never home," it's good to rethink your distribution of time and presence.[ix]

This being said, there is a great need for global-scale contribution today. The awesome part is that the best contribution most of us can make is from our homes. Support your extended family, friends, and your community by being a role model. Stay home and spread positivity into the world online. Help those who don't have the luxury of staying home, like doctors, shop clerks, cops, bankers, and other heroes who work hard to save our asses by not getting infected and not spreading any infection.

If our main needs are not met, we start exhibiting dysfunctional behavioral patterns. It is essential to understand what our main human needs are and work towards meeting them even in isolation.

How to Take Care of Yourself and Deal with Loneliness

This is not a time to make big, life-altering decisions, huge changes, or big plans. This is a time to turn inwards, get to know yourself, and ground yourself. I know that so many of you are going through so many challenges, so much hardship. The world literally turned into a place we never imagined. Or actually, some of us did imagine it, and we exported this imagination in the form of some catastrophe movie. But now we're experiencing something eerily similar to these movies in our own skin. And that's scary.

We are more anxious than normal. Maybe we're busier than normal. Maybe we feel more detached from our emotions to try to compensate for the anxiety we feel. This is why it is more important than ever to find time for ourselves, to be quiet, to listen to what our heart says. If you're not in a good headspace, you won't be able to help anyone else.

Isolation can give birth to a deep sense of loneliness. I know it is extremely hard being separated from your family right now, being denied of your friends' company. Maybe you're stuck alone now and you've never lived alone before. Maybe you've been separated from your love. Maybe you are stuck in a country you traveled to but couldn't leave in time. Maybe you are battling this insidious virus at the moment, being quarantined and monitored. It is very hard to be in all of these situations.

When we are scared and lonely, the first thing we crave is company, a pat on our shoulder, a warm hug… But unfortunately, at the moment, the best we can do is social distancing. However, we don't need to wither in this condition. We can find a way to learn and grow under such circumstances as well. Let me share with you how we can do social distancing in a healthy, supporting, self-caring way. Let's stay in a good place mentally and physically.

Before I share with you some of the best practices I use to stay sane, let me point something out to you. In conventional speaking, the concepts of loneliness and solitude are used as synonyms. But by definition they mean two different things.

Loneliness is a state of being when our needs for company and connection are unmet. Solitude doesn't necessarily imply negative emotions arising from unmet social needs. In solitude, one is satisfactory company for themselves. This is a big difference. In solitude, you can be joyful, even powerful. Solitude is a positive experience.

Being physically alone used to be dangerous in prehistoric times. Even today we associate the state of being alone as something negative, and therefore, we rush to attach the label "lonely" to our experience. But it doesn't have to be that way. We can find meaning and fulfillment when we are alone and transform our experience into solitude. It is basically a mental switch. We can flip this switch by, one, getting familiar with the difference between loneliness and solitude; two, becoming open to consciously perceiving our experience of aloneness as solitude rather than loneliness; and three, learning practices that help us enable that mental switch.

We as a society have the tendency to label people who are alone as loners, weirdos, or anti-socials; being alone, therefore, has a negative priming effect by default. The fear of being a social outcast also adds to the negative side of the equation of being alone. Feeling lonely can trigger a sense of lacking, a sense of deficiency in us.

I want to help you recognize that being alone is actually not a weakness, but a strength. You will feel more empowered, resilient, and content if you can embrace your experience of solitude. Those who can be alone with themselves and have it as a positive experience are comfortable with themselves.

How Do You Flip the Switch from Loneliness to Solitude?

We sometimes feel lonely because we think others are somewhere doing something cool and we aren't. Well, for the first time, that's not true. No one's anywhere. No one's doing anything. We're all isolated. Globally. We are all locked up in—optimally—our homes waiting for this crisis to end.

The feeling of loneliness can also come from thoughts such as, "I need my love to feel safe," or, "I need my father's company to feel secure." These are all absolutely normal reactions to isolation. It is important to acknowledge and understand these feelings. But it's also important to understand that this crisis is an opportunity to get better acquainted with yourself. This can be the time when you consciously focus on becoming the person you want to be. You can become it.

Practice 1

Look into the mirror and observe each little corner of your face. How does it feel when looking deep into your own eyes? How do you talk to yourself in the morning? Notice it. How do you talk to yourself when you're annoyed at someone?

Understand where your emotions and thoughts are stemming from. We so wish other people to understand us, to accept us. But how can we expect that when we don't understand and accept ourselves? This is the time to solve that big puzzle.

Learn to articulate yourself effectively to others by first doing it to yourself. Tell yourself your self-discoveries in the mirror. How does it feel? Do you feel awkward? Cringy? Why? Are you comfortable talking to yourself about yourself? Why? Get curious.

The first time I did this exercise, I burst into laughter. I felt so weird for talking to my reflection like that. Then I looked around to see if anybody saw that I was not only talking to myself, but also laughing. Surprise! Nobody saw it. The perks of living in isolation.

The second time I tried to talk about myself I started crying. And I cried for a good twenty minutes. I wept for the things I should have sheltered myself from, for the innocent and helpless girl I was a few years ago. I wept for the helplessness I was feeling in those moments. What I feel now. And it felt liberating. I understood—again—that a deep fear of abandonment will be my constant companion probably for life. But I also knew that this fear is just an emotion feeding itself from an old memory. That, while I feel abandoned, and based on my early life it is actually a very reasonable thing to feel, I am not abandoned in reality. My love is about to come home from work. (Yes, I am the lucky one who got stuck with her partner. I can't put in words how grateful I am for that.)

Practice 2

Write in your journal. Let your soul flow through the pen and note all your emotions, states of mind, day by day. Release, let go of your troubles on paper. You don't need to write eloquently, just get it out of your head. Feelings of loneliness arise when we're in our heads, and the only way of getting out of there is to do something physical, tangible. Journaling is such an action because you give a physical, visible shape to intangible thoughts. Seeing your thoughts in front of you can help you understand them better and see them from a different perspective.

To those who absolutely detest writing, record your thoughts with a voice recording app. I did this countless times. It was a great conflict de-escalation tool when I did long distance with my boyfriend. Before I brought my impulsive problems to him, I recorded them with my phone. Thanks to the distance and time difference, I had to wait a few hours before talking to him. One or two hours after I recorded my thoughts I listened to them again. In the majority of the cases, it felt as if someone else said those words and had those feelings. Listening to my past self in a moment when I was in calmer mood was eye opening. I ended up talking to my boyfriend about zero of the issues I recorded. But I enjoy listening to my own voice notes even months later. They are important reminders and lessons.

You can record (or journal) snappy, angry thoughts, deep thoughts, sad, soul-tearing thoughts—this is a healthy practice regardless. It helps you get to know and understand yourself. No emotion is good or bad. They just are. As long as you can calmly observe them, let them be, and when the time comes, let them go, there's nothing wrong with *feeling*. Problems arise when you engage in self-harming activities because of your emotions. Or if you harm others. The problem doesn't lie within the emotion but instead the action we choose to take. Observing, allowing, and releasing emotions is a difficult skill, but it can be learned. Meditation and mindfulness practices can help you a lot. I will share some ideas about it later in this book.

Thanks to my voice notes, I learned to choose patience about sharing the first impulsive thoughts that popped in my mind. I learned about myself that I'm emotionally reactive to stimuli that poke on my overly anxious emotional memory bank. And I also learned that in a neutral state of mind I would not want to talk about these annoyances because they are not the result of someone doing something wrong. They are just my old wounds itching, and nobody can soothe them but me. Even if I decide to mention something, it is much more constructive to do it when calm. But I know for sure that I wouldn't be able to find peace and security in someone else's words until I find it in myself.

So record your thoughts, either in written or audio form. Read or listen to yourself objectively. Assess your problem and give yourself advice just as you'd do if your best friend shared their problem with you. You have great advice to dispense—as I'm sure you've done to your friends so many times. Just learn to listen to yourself just as you'd listen to a friend. This is how you build the practice of understanding yourself.

Practice 3

Find out what you like to do the most in your own company.

Do you know what you like to do on your own? Do you enjoy preparing your coffee in the morning? Do you love getting lost in an adventure novel? What do you like to do when you're by yourself?

It's important to ask yourself what you can do each day that brings you joy. If you learn what brings you joy—truly—it's a gift nothing and no one can take away from you. It is a gift from yourself to yourself. This is a great time to try more things that you suspect you'd like and see what you actually like doing. See what connects with you, test it out. What do you like doing in your own space?

If you conclude that you like doing things together with people, you can still do that. You just need to get a little bit creative. Write someone a letter. Record funny little video snippets for your loved ones. Send someone a grateful voice recording.

When we think about being together with people, in fact, we're looking for a connection, an emotion, an experience—not necessarily the physical presence. Often when we're together with a lot of people, we feel drained rather than energized. Try to identify what experience and what emotions you're seeking from a person you can't be together with and try to recreate that ambience online. You can create virtual routines with your friends. You can start watching a movie at the same time. Cook the same thing and share the experience on video chat. You can listen to the same podcast and discuss your take on it over the phone.

I don't want to downplay the importance of physical presence. No phone can replicate a warm hug, a squeeze of your shoulder. But you don't have to be robbed of all the warm and fuzzy experiences socializing can give, either. Create the shared experience even if you don't share the space. Involve people in activities you used to do alone virtually. Use your social media to spread loving, kind messages into the world. You can do so much to connect with others on so many levels!

In Italy, people living in the same block of flats sang together, each on their own balcony. A personal trainer gave free sport classes from a rooftop to the surrounding inhabitants. There are so many ways we can serve and be useful. Find out what your superpower is! These times can really reveal the best of humanity. They can show the worst of us, too. But also the best. Let's work on the latter.

Practice 4

If you have access to nature where you can do social distancing properly, allow yourself some time every day to go. Take a deep breath of fresh air. Identify the smell of the trees, the grass. Listen to the wind blowing, birds chirping, bugs buzzing. Nature is alive. Look at the beauty of spring, which is just at the point of full blooming. Nature hasn't changed. Spring is still coming. Take refuge in that. Take in the hopeful and beautiful. Allow yourself to enjoy the peace of green fields, the majestic mountains, or the restless ocean waves. Nature is alive and so are you. Feel it.

Today, I took my bike and went down to the beach. It was a lovely afternoon. You could see people scattered on the sandy plains. It made me very happy to see that everybody was taking the six-feet distancing seriously. I practiced yoga for thirty minutes kissed by the sun, hearing the ocean waves slowly hitting the pier of Manhattan Beach. I heard people laughing in the distance. The sand felt warm and comforting. Digging my feet deep in it filled my heart with gratitude. Such simple things we failed to appreciate before. Seeing and feeling the ocean breeze after seven days of staying in my house felt like redemption. If you have the chance to spend time in nature where there are not many people, go and do it. For your own sanity.

Also, try to create inviting, pleasant surroundings in your home. Make order, reorganize your shelves. Create yourself a home you enjoy looking at, smelling, and hearing. This is the perfect time to buy that air freshener, those indoor plants. Play some mellow, background piano songs. Make your home inviting.

Surround yourself with beauty and humor. Place different Post-it Notes around the house reminding yourself about self-care, self-love, and self-acceptance. Write motivational quotes. Place your spouse's sweet notes in a visible place. Put a photo of your loved ones on your nightstand so you see them first thing in the morning.

Chapter 3—How to Deal with Uncertainty

"Uncertainty is the only certainty there is, and knowing how to live with insecurity is the only security." — John Allen Paulos

In the previous chapter, I mentioned that some people are wired to thrive in uncertainty. However, they are a wild minority. Most of us hit the panic button once uncertainty arises, and we crawl back into our beds with a jar of Nutella and want to hear no more about it. As much as I love my bed and Nutella, I must surrender to the fact that there are better ways to deal with ambiguity.

Uncertainty is an essential part of life. We can't escape it, so a more healthy coping strategy can be acceptance. If it comes easily to you, great. But for the planners, fixers, perfectionists, and saviors of the world out there, acceptance requires conscious and deliberate practice. We can't plan our way to everything. We don't know what to plan for.

One aspect of practicing acceptance is being okay with your feelings about uncertainty. If you experience worry, stress, fear, anxiety... those are all normal reactions to uncertain times, so give yourself permission to feel them. Don't run away from these heavy emotions, don't try to numb them. Notice them, give them space, observe them as a part of the human experience. I usually do an imagery meditation when feelings of anxiety, fear, or doubt pop up. I imagine myself kneeling at the bank of a river holding a basket in my lap. I name the emotion while breathing deeply, "anxiety," "worry," "fear." Then I imagine putting this emotion into the basket. (My mind is simple. I just imagine the written word of anxiety, let's say, being put in the basket. Nothing complicated.) Then I put the basket with the emotion in it on the fast-flowing river in front of me and I witness as the current washes the basket away. Sometimes it is enough to do this practice once. Sometimes I need to do it over and over again.

You can also write down your worries. Research shows that writing down our troubles helps us move through them with more ease.

Gratitude is another antidote to negative emotions arising from uncertainty. It is hard to stay grateful in such times because our brain's natural tendency to focus on what can go wrong is highly activated. It is a natural human reaction. So is fear. We learned to fear the uncertain to survive, after all. Negativity bias and fear can interact like oil on fire. We spill into a vicious loop of fear of negative outcomes, which make us even more fearful.

Did you see the movie *The Lord of the Rings*? There is a scene where the heroes are hopelessly fighting to no avail with the orcs—the disfigured, monstrous enemies. When they are about to get overpowered by the orcs, Gandalf the White riding his horse slays through the evil crowd, shining like a bright, white star, blinding the orcs. Gratitude acts the same way. The beam of a grateful thought can slay fear and negativity. Where there is gratitude, anxiety and fear cannot survive.

To practice focusing on the sunny side, write down three things you're grateful for within all the uncertainty. You can think of anything, but make your grateful statements specific. When you write them down, pause for a moment to appreciate them. Enjoy the warm, fuzzy feelings they trigger in you. Where do you feel gratitude in your body? Identify it. Most people feel warmth around their heart. I usually feel butterflies in my stomach. Use this mind-body connection practice to help your brain pause its negativity spiral.

Researchers proved that by simply thinking about something you're grateful for, you'll release happiness neurochemicals such as serotonin and dopamine. These will give you a mood boost, and encouragement to your brain to keep looking for things to appreciate.

Krazy kindness. Yes, I wrote the crazy with a k on purpose. Just for fun. I intend to start a krazy kindness movement. Who's with me? Kindness has a magical quality. It is intended to help, cheer up, support, and appreciate someone else, but while practiced, it reflects the given benefits back to us. When you give love to someone, you yourself will feel the love. When you cheer up someone, you yourself will be merrier. Try it.

When we feel anxious or worried, we can lock ourselves in our head and ruminate. We need to practice getting out of our head. How? By connecting to people doing small, intentional acts of kindness.

Ask a friend about how they're doing. Smile and say thank you to the cashier who is still working. Pause to admire your spouse's drawing and compliment them rather than rushing past it. Positive interactions with others make us happier. Our brain releases oxytocin when we practice krazy kindness, which makes us feel supported when we're going through uncertain times.

Build resilience by finding meaning and a sense of a bigger why. What are you hoping for once this uncertain period is over? For example, if you were about to get married but you had to postpone the wedding, think about why you were doing the wedding in the first place. It is for the celebration of love you and your partner share. Did that essence disappear? No. The wedding got postponed and you're in the middle of a global mess. Use this challenging time by experiencing a new level of togetherness. If you and your future spouse can survive a season of quarantine with love and mutual support, you gain further assurance that you are making the right step. What is the meaning of marriage, anyway? Mutual support and love. Through good and bad. Recalling the meaning certain actions hold for us helps us through challenges.

Take time to think about and write down what sense of meaning there is for you during this pandemic. What pumps your motivation? What are your hopes for the future? Keep them in mind and work towards them.

Explore the magic of daily rituals. In times of uncertainty, having a set of consistent rituals can make a big difference. These little points of certainty can ground you when everything seems elusive. Don't think about anything fancy here. To me my daily grounding rituals are my ten-minute meditation practice, my morning coffee, listening to my confidence-boosting affirmations, and listening to at least one educational podcast.

Choose a few activities that help you find comfort and stability. To come up with the rituals-to-be, ask yourself these questions: What activity makes me feel centered? What gives me comfort when there's a lot going on? Find at least two short activities that you can commit to doing every day. This will create a sense of stability, even in uncertain times. To me it doesn't matter what's happening, at eight in the morning I'm preparing and drinking my coffee. I do not care; I don't compromise on that. The coffee time is me time.

Change expectations of plans and stay flexible. Expectations in times of uncertainty are a Molotov cocktail for disappointment. You can expect to do something, to be somewhere, to achieve something next April, but it may not happen. You can't control outcomes. Expecting the worst sets us up for over-caution, and we may not even try to do what we want. Expecting the best is purely wishful thinking, and the best is a category that reality rarely lives up to.

The best we can do is to have a crystal clear idea of an outcome we want to experience and then use what's within our control to make conscious steps towards reaching that outcome. I only make plans about things I can influence, like planning when to call my mom, when to meditate, when to work. But I also am aware that even these plans may get pushed back or they might not even happen at all. My mom may be in the shower when I call. I might not have time to meditate at ten in the morning because the repairman came over. I might not work today because I have a terrible headache.

Be prepared for different outcome possibilities. In times of uncertainty, we lose our sense of control. We feel like a plastic bag caught up in the wind. I'm an absolute control freak. I need safety and security in my life, otherwise I'm constantly anxious. Right now I'm stuck in Los Angeles, which is not the worst place to be, but I have a limited time here due to my visa's restrictions. I need to leave in a few months. Where? Back to

Europe where coronavirus is in its heyday? Latin America is shut down. Asia is shut down. New Zealand is shut down. I didn't check Africa, but I think it must be the same. I can't plan where I'm going to live, what city, what area... or how I'll manage to stay together with my boyfriend. It's unnerving. But what can I do?

All I can do is make a list of possible places I'd gladly live in, write a checklist of the neighborhood, the type of apartment, amenities I'd like to have... "Plan for the possibilities and stay flexible" is my new motto.

All we can and should do is plan multiple optimal life routes—not just about moving, about anything. And then, having clear, written plans, start working toward realizing one of them. Embrace if you hit a roadblock and have to diverge to another plan, and then work on that.

The truth is, there is never certainty. It's an illusion that we have control. What we have is information about predictability—in some cases we can predict certain outcomes with a higher accuracy than in other times. In 2020, predictability is at a record low. That's all. But if we felt in total control in 2019, well, we were delusional.

This being said, it is important to have a sense of security in our everyday life, otherwise we'd all get a heart attack at the age of twenty. Imagine not feeling safe going out on the street, thinking there is a fifty percent chance you'll die. Who would go out, ever? Or imagine being uncertain about the food you buy in the supermarket. Or that your car will explode once you press the ignition with a 75% probability. Right? We wouldn't do anything and would constantly stress. But we know intuitively that going out and walking on the street is safe. Some people die walking the street, but they are the exception. (In more peaceful parts of the world, anyways.) We know that the produce we buy at the market is not poisonous. Or that cars don't explode just like that. Most things in life are usually predictable and safe—so much so that we don't even think about them.

Add a highly contagious virus to this equation, which has a steeper mortality rate than its virus cousins, and everything goes berserk. Now we do contemplate the chances of getting contaminated or dying if we go out on the street (especially folks above 60 or those with immune system problems). Now we do think about the safety of the vegetables and fruits we buy at the supermarket. What if someone with COVID-19 sneezed on them? We touch them with gloves (as we always should have). We wash the soul out of them (as we always should have). The world transformed into this utopic crazyland, turning predictable safe things we didn't even think about into dangerous life hazards.

It's scary. And mind blowing. And it is the new reality for now. What are we going to do about it? A healthy, new goal we could add to our life would be accepting our current reality. Because once we do it, magically, it becomes more predictable, less uncertain. The certainty is that it is uncertain. But we can expect that now with a high probability. This is the paradox of acceptance. Once we calm our mind and accept the unchangeable, the unpredictable, we'll be mentally prepared.

It is much healthier to say, "Yes, I don't know what tomorrow will bring, but I am ready for it because it will come regardless if I'm ready or not," than to say, "I so, so, so wish that this virus goes away just as quickly as it came, that restaurants will open next month and everything will be back to normal." It's okay to keep the latter as a heartfelt best-case scenario, but don't settle on it as The Reality. You'll be disappointed, and an unexpected negative change will knock you even lower.

Counterintuitively, accepting a negative experience is in itself a positive experience. Accepting that painful things can happen will free you from a lot of anxiety and will shift your focus from "what if" to "then what?" I'm sorry to summon the Black List of possible negative outcomes, but it is important to stay realistic and prepare ourselves mentally.

- I might die.
- Someone I love might die.
- Someone I know might die.
- I might get sick.
- Someone I love might get sick.
- Someone I know might get sick.
- I might lose my job.
- I might not have a stable income.
- I won't have childcare, a good, stable education for my children.

- I can't make any plans.
- The stock market might take years to recover.
- We won't be able to leave our home and will need to practice social distancing for long months or years.
- We can't get together with friends, go to social gatherings, work alongside coworkers, or celebrate life events.
- We may be fearful to be close to other people, getting touched.
- We get fed up by our partner, children, friends we're locked together with.
- We can't get out of a random country.
- Things will never be the same as before.
- Things will go back to the same as before.

These fears are real—they affect our mind. Trying to force them out of our psyche is not the best solution. The more we fight a thought, the more power it will have over us. The key here is not denial but understanding, preparation. We will go through this list in the next chapter and we'll look at possible ways to manage the fears mentioned better. The list is not exhaustive, by any means. If you have a fear I didn't mention, just notice how I approach mellowing it and do the same for yourself.

I strongly suggest you not ruminate on the things mentioned in the list. Getting entangled or staying totally oblivious facing such outcomes are both cocktails for disaster. We need to acknowledge that there is a probability for any of them to happen. There always has been a probability for any of these things mentioned on the Black List to happen, just right now the percentage of the probability climbed up one or two steps. That's all. The more we acknowledge and accept this fact, the more likely we'll respect safety requirements, appreciate our health and the health and presence of people dear to us, feel grateful to have a job, be resourceful in finding alternative income streams in case we lose our job, and try being the best version of ourselves like our life depended on it.

Become aware of your feelings. It is not the uncertainty that bugs me necessarily; more so my tendency to get lost in my emotions about it. It is a thin line between embracing and accepting your negative emotions and indulging in them. The question of, "How will I be together with my boyfriend after I have spent my visa limit?" can easily turn into, "What if, once we're separated, he'll distance himself because he knows there is no hope for traveling to be allowed at a normal rate, and he'll have someone else in the US while fearing to tell me about it so as to not be responsible for my reckless exposure to coronavirus out of love-deprivation depression? Better break up with him now and save myself from all the emotional pain and coronavirus."

Right? The mind can get to exaggerated, wildly dark places. My point is that speculation leads to emotions, which can lead to more speculation and then more emotions. To stop the cycle it can be helpful to recognize the emotion—in my case, fear of abandonment—and then remind myself that I can't predict the future, but I can help create it by fostering positive emotions about what's possible. For example, I could talk to my boyfriend about what we can do after my visa expires—in theory. I still have some months left, and so much can change during that time. We can find a country that allows traveling and live on our savings for a few months until I can come back to the US again. We can find a country where both of us could work and stay there until the coronavirus craze wears out. We could always move to Romania and live there for six months. There are possibilities. Which will be available at the critical point? We don't know yet. But as I mentioned before, it is better to have some plans lined out and stay flexible. We also need to be prepared that we'll be separated for some time. We can figure out how to cope with it once that future becomes certain.

Until then, it is just a very worst-case scenario we should acknowledge but shouldn't ruminate on.

Build your coping and adapting skills. To be clear, this isn't synonymous with expecting the worst. It's more about self-confidence; you being able to handle any difficulty life might throw at you.

Have you heard about the concept of defensive pessimism? It means considering the worst and then planning how you'd manage it. Research shows that this can actually help people deal with anxiety.[x] "What's the worst that can happen?"

In my case, the worst would be if we're separated indefinitely. It would be emotionally very challenging, but we would survive it. We could video call each other every day. We could constantly search for ways to be together. We could stay busy working. If we're not together, it means it's because the world is still in quarantine.

There's not much more to do anyway but work, plan, and watch Netflix.

Take preemptive measures to reduce stress. When we feel uncertain about the future, some stress accumulates in our body—even if we don't feel stressed. Over time, this can turn into high blood pressure, muscle tension, high cholesterol levels, and other physical manifestations.

Mindfulness meditation and yoga are amazing stress reduction techniques. Just a few minutes of practice daily can do magic. Mindfulness can be a helpful ally in your anxiety reduction. I regularly practice mindfulness meditation for almost two years now. In the beginning, I was honestly convinced that it wouldn't help me to sit in silence, trying to accept and let go of my thoughts. For weeks I was practicing, and since I was very dedicated, I made some improvements in not scratching my backside when it was itching; just calmly noticing the sensation, not judging the event, just say *itching* and then breathe in and breathe out the experience without being reactive. I also observed what obsessive thoughts popped up in my mind when I sat in silence—which were the ones that left easily, and which were the ones that needed more embracing.

Without noticing, I became better at releasing negative, anxious thoughts, even the ones that seemed the scariest at the time. Just kept returning to my breath over and over again without judgment. Slowly I got more familiar with how my brain works, and since I was in a silent, undisturbed place I could practice some metacognition—thinking about my thoughts. Meditation opened my thinking brain to my observing brain. It was a slow process, I didn't wake up the second day feeling "I know myself." My intention wasn't even to get to know myself when I started meditating, rather, I wanted to become less reactive.

Decreased reactivity is another great byproduct of meditation, by the way. The first time I felt how beneficial my regular daily practice was, was on a Saturday afternoon, about seven months into meditating. My ex said something that normally would have triggered a kneejerk reaction in me, but not this time. There was a brief moment where somewhere in the back of my brain I translated the emotion into words: "irritation." And immediately I fired out a command: "breathe." And so I did. You know those scenes in a movie where the main character experiences some kind of cathartic discovery and the camera starts zooming in on them while the outside noises and sights become blurry and toned down? That's exactly how I felt. He kept talking, but I stopped paying attention to him. This experience to me was a huge step. It was the catalyst of my shifting beliefs about myself. I used to tell myself, "I'm emotionally reactive, that's who I am. I can't do anything about that." And in that moment I first learned about myself... "Yes, I can."

To me, meditation was and is a life-altering skill. It empowered me, helped me shed some unhelpful beliefs about myself, I could manage my anxiety better, and it opened up the gates to mental peace. I honestly hope it can do that for you, too.

Meditation Practice

Try this simple practice now. Put down the book after you read the instructions and just do it. Sit down comfortably on a cushion or chair. Straighten your back, sit stable and tall. Rest your hands gently in your lap. When you feel ready, close your eyes. Take a deep breath in. Follow your breath as it enters your nostrils, as it flows down your throat and fills up your lungs. Give thanks for your lungs, which do a lot of work in keeping you alive. Notice the tiny pause when your inhalation turns into an exhalation. Follow your exhalation as it leaves your body. Repeat this sequence about ten times. If a thought pops up in your mind, don't get discouraged. Calmly note "thinking" and then put it in a basket and let it flow down the river. Continue following your breath.

When you feel that you are calm and centered enough, continue your practice with a visualization practice. Feel the ground where your legs and feet touch it. Absorb it. Find your roots in it. Now, imagine that you are still and grounded like a mountain. I think all of us can recall how Kilimanjaro looks like. Imagine that you are massive, strong, peaceful, and still like Mount Kilimanjaro. Bring the image of the mountain in your body. Imagine that you are the mountain. Strong and grounded. Nothing can move you. Nothing can break you. Wind, storm, it doesn't matter, the mountain doesn't surrender to any of them. Inhale deeply to the roots of the mountain, exhale slowly, and let go of your fears. You're a mountain. Inhale deeply and fill you body with positive, empowering energy. Exhale and release your anxiety.

Continue this practice for ten to fifteen minutes. When you're done, observe how you feel compared to the beginning of this meditation practice. Do you feel stronger, more stable, relieved, lighter? However you feel, it's okay. If you don't feel a physical change, that's okay, too. Just accept what is for now. If you feel a positive shift in you, bring that energy into your day.

When you ruminate about a tomorrow that's outside of your circle of influence, you're sacrificing what's happening right now on the altar of judging what hasn't happened yet. Mindfulness helps you notice and appreciate the beauty in the moment. Work on not getting trapped in a fear-driven thought cycle about the unknowable future.

While meditation is the best way to become more present, there are other approaches, too. Like gratitude. It helps me stay more positive and present when I think about what was good today. Not knowing what tomorrow brings doesn't have to be scary or bad. Today, I can do whatever I want. I can write, read, watch a movie, embrace my loved ones (if they are close), and I can connect with people I miss over the internet.

Move your focus on what you can control. Don't overlook the little things you can do to make your life better. The worst we can do is obsess about the big things we can't control—like this pandemic.

Chapter 4—How to Deal with Anxiety

When we experience a lack of control in our lives, we feel anxious and despaired. Finding meaning or purpose for ourselves becomes a real challenge. And, if we spend a long time in this state, we begin to break down mentally and physically. Therefore, it is essential to be able to recognize, sit with, accept, and eventually release these emotions.

Anxiety, being hyper vigilant, being afraid—these brain quirks worked perfectly eons ago. When our ancestors entered unfamiliar territory and didn't know who or what might be lurking behind the bushes, their overwhelming caution ensured survival. But today, this kneejerk reaction, which hasn't evolved, is a hindrance in everyday life.

When we encounter some uncertainty, our brains push us to overreact.

Some people are able to override this brain quirk and shift their thinking in a more rational direction. This requires presence, mental toughness, and emotional intelligence. When you have a sound base of emotional intelligence, you get good at standing still in the face of uncertainty—despite your brain fighting against it. We can get better at handling our emotions that are clouding our judgment.

The limbic system is the part of our brain that responds to uncertainty with an automatized fear reaction. Fear leaves little room for good decision-making. When we're good at dealing with uncertainty, we become aware of this fear. We spot it as soon as it begins and we can contain it before it gets out of control. The antidote to one's fears is naming those fears. Say the fear you have in your mind out loud. Remind yourself that this is a scheme of your limbic system. It wants to help you, but the poor thing is stuck in like 100, 000 BCE. Remember that the primitive part of our brain is trying to overpower the logical part. Thereby I summon the Black List again to practice naming our fears. I will group them into umbrella topics and we will discuss them in the following pages.

Fear of Death

- I might die.
- Someone I love might die.
- Someone I know might die.
- I might get sick.
- Someone I love might get sick.
- Someone I know might get sick.

Fear of Financial Loss

- I might lose my job.
- I might not have a stable income.

- The stock market might take years to recover.

Fear of Losing Connection

- We won't be able to leave our home and will need to practice social distancing for long months or years.
- We can't get together with friends, go to social gatherings, work alongside coworkers, or celebrate life events.
- We get fed up by our partner, children, friends we're locked together with.
- We may be fearful of being close to other people, getting touched.

Existential Crises

- I won't have childcare, a good, stable education for my children.
- I can't make any plans.
- We can't get out of a random country.

- Things will never be the same as before.
- Things will go back to the same as before.

Heavy stuff. Let's get started.

Fear of Death

This is the most ancient, most rudimental fear of humanity. All of our basic instincts are aligned to avoid this one outcome: dying. Feeling that we are in imminent, uncontrollable danger is crippling. A global pandemic with its worrisome statistics, strict, unprecedented safety measures, and incessant news broadcasts can very likely trigger fear. Even if we're in the age group where death rates are negligible (although every death is a tragedy, and survivors may suffer a lot having COVID-19), most of us have mothers and fathers, grandmothers and grandfathers, aunts and uncles, teachers, and friends who may be facing a higher risk of a bad outcome if they get infected.

Fear of getting sick, losing a loved one, or our own life, therefore, is neither crazy nor irrational. Still, in many ways, too much fear restricts our lives. It imprisons us. Fear can also be used as a tool of oppression, manipulation, and bad deeds; people can be made to do or not do a lot of things out of fear. Therefore, it is essential on some level to be able to understand, embrace, and soothe our fears. Even the most rudimentary ones. How do we walk the path of fear?

1. Approach the fear of death as a Buddhist.

In Buddhist teachings, we can read that the main cause of our suffering and anxiety is ignorance of the nature of reality, and craving and clinging to illusory things. We can call this ego, and ego thrives on fear. Our goal here is to release a little bit the tight grip of craving and clinging. I would like to share with you a Dharma talk from Thich

Nhat Hanh, a Zen Master and Buddhist teacher, on how to let go of all attachments.

"Let us practice like this. Breathing in, I know that this body is not me. Breathing out, I feel I am not caught in this body. In fact, they begin with eyes. These eyes are not me. I am not caught by these eyes. Eyes, ears, nose, tongue, body, and mind— six things. They always begin with eyes. Breathing in, I know that these eyes are not me. I am not caught in these eyes. I am life without boundaries. These eyes have a beginning. These eyes can disintegrate, but I am not caught in these eyes. They begin with the eyes and continue with the nose, the ears, the tongue, the body, and the mind.

Then they switch to the objects of the six senses. These forms are not me. I am not caught in these forms. These sounds are not me. I am not caught in these sounds. Because the dying person may be attached to forms, sounds, body, mind, et cetera, considering these things to be self, considering that they are losing these, they are losing self.

After having meditated on the six senses and their objects and the six kinds of consciousnesses, they begin to meditate on the four elements. Breathing in, I know the element water is in me. Breathing out, I know that the element water is not me. I am not caught in the element of water. When you breathe and you meditate like that, you see that the water is everywhere, around you, inside of you. Water is not you. You are more than water. You are not caught by the element of water.

And you meditate also on the element of heat. The heat in me is not me. I am not caught by the heat in me. The heat is everywhere. You do not consider the heat to be yourself. Breathing in I realize the element of earth in me. Breathing out, I know that I am not the earth. The element earth is not me and I am not caught in the element called earth. So they continue like that with the elements air, with the four elements.

And they come to the five aggregates we have learned in the last few days: form, feelings, perceptions, mental formations and consciousness. Breathing in, I know that form is not me. I am not limited by form. Feelings are not me. I am not limited by feelings. Perceptions are not me. I am not caught by the perceptions. Mental formations are not me. I am not these mental formations. Consciousness is not me. I am not caught by this consciousness. Then they practice looking into the nature of causes and conditions? […]

These lines may be a little bit abstract to you, but it is possible for all of us to get a deep understanding, a deep experience of it. You have to know the true nature of death, the true nature of dying, in order to understand really the true nature of living. If you don't understand what is death, you don't understand what is life, also. Therefore, it is very important to know the nature of birth and death. The teaching of the Buddha is to relieve us of suffering and the base of suffering is ignorance, ignorance about the true nature of yourself, of things around you. Since you don't understand, you are too afraid and fear has brought you a lot of suffering. That is why the offering of non-fear is the best kind of offering you can make to someone."[xi]

While Thich Nhat Hahn's words may sound hard to grasp and even harder to follow, we can find some solace in the idea of nonattachment and non-fear. Death and illness are natural byproducts of the human existence. We talk about certain aspects of human existence like life, death, self, but rarely do we have a real understanding of the meaning of these words. To the word death, for example, we attach the meaning of existing in one moment and ceasing to be in another. Also, we consider birth as the beginning. Being born means that from nothing we become something. That is how we, the Western society, look at birth and death. Buddhist teachings invite us to look at these moments differently; to shift our idea and thus our fear of dying, our fear of ceasing to exist.

The Zen Master continues his teaching presenting the Buddhist idea of birth and death as follows:

"You may think that the sheet of paper has a birthday and will have a day of dying. We may imagine a day when the piece of paper is produced from nothing, it suddenly becomes something, a sheet of paper. Is it possible? When you look into the sheet of paper in this very moment, you don't have to go back to someday. Just look at it in the present moment. Into the true nature of the paper you see what? You see that the piece of paper is made of non-paper elements. This is a very scientific way of looking, because you don't accept anything that is not evident.

When I touch the sheet of paper, I touch the tree, the forest, because I know that deep inside there is the existence of the trees, the forest. If you return the element tree back to the forest, the sheet of paper cannot be here. Right? I also touch the sunshine. Even at midnight touching the sheet of paper, I touch sunshine. Because sunshine is one element called non-paper elements that has made up the paper. Because without sunshine, no tree can grow. So touching the tree, I touch the sunshine.

I touch the cloud. There is a cloud floating in this sheet of paper. You don't have to be a poet to see the cloud in a sheet of paper. Because without a cloud, there would be no rain and no forest can grow. So the cloud is in there. The trees are in there. The sunshine, the minerals from the earth, the earth, time, space, people, insects—everything in the cosmos seem to be existing in this sheet of paper. If you look deeply, you find that everything in the cosmos is present in this moment in the sheet of paper. If you send one of these elements back to its source, the paper would not be there. That is why it is very important to see that a sheet of paper is made of, only of, non-paper elements. Our body is like that also.

So is it possible to say that from nothing, something has come into existence? From nothing, can you have something? No. Because before we perceive it as a sheet of paper, it had been sunshine. It had been trees. It had been clouds. The paper hasn't come from nothing: *Rien ne se crée.* Nothing has been created. The day you believe to be the birthday of the sheet of paper is something we call a continuation day. Before that day, it had been something else, many things even, and on that day it was perceived as a sheet of paper. So the next time, when you celebrate your birthday, instead of singing happy birthday, you sing happy continuation day. We have done that to a number of friends. Happy continuation day.

The true nature of this sheet of paper, is the nature of no-birth: *Rien ne se crée, rien ne se perd.*[1] Our true nature is also the nature of no-birth. Our birth certificate is misleading. It was certified that we were born on that day from such and such hospital or city. We accepted to begin to be on that day, but we know very well that we had been there in the womb of our mother long before that. From nothing, how can you become something? From no one, how can you become someone? Even before the day of your conception in your mother, you had been there. In your father, in your mother, and everywhere else, also. So if you try to go back, you cannot find a beginning of you. You have been there for a long time and everywhere.

People think they can eliminate what they don't want: they can burn, they can kill. But it's not by destroying that they can reduce something to

---

[1] "Nothing is born and nothing can die." Antoine Lavoisier

nothing. They killed Mahatma Gandhi. They shot Martin Luther King. But these people continue to be among us in many forms and their being continues. Their spirit continues.

Let us now try to eliminate this sheet of paper. Let us try to burn it to see whether we are capable of making it into nothing. […]

Ash is what you can see. If you have observed, you see that some smoke has come up and that is a continuation of the sheet of paper. Now the sheet of paper has become part of a cloud in the sky. You may meet it again tomorrow in the form of a raindrop on your forehead. But maybe you will not be mindful and you will not know that this is a meeting. You may think that the raindrop is foreign to you, but it may just be the sheet of paper into which you have practiced looking deeply. The way it is now, is it nothing? No, I don't think the sheet of paper has become nothing. Part of it has become the cloud. You can say,

"Goodbye, see you again one day in one form or another."[xii]

I invite you to read the teaching of Thich Nhat Hahn whenever you feel down, whenever you feel like the fear of death is overwhelming you. Sit with your discomfort and meditate on the six senses proposed by the Zen Master. These eyes are not me, these hands are not me…

Try to embrace an alternative way of looking at the world. A way that keeps you more grounded, more happy, more at peace. Because what is to happen is going to happen whether you worry or not. It doesn't matter how many nails you bite off due to anxiety, how many hours you spend obsessing about what ifs—by doing these things, you won't change anything except your blood pressure.

Washing your hands, staying at home, distancing socially, doing the best you can, spreading accurate information to your family, these things help much more. Staying mentally stable, decreasing that tremendous fear of loss that works in your heart—in the heart of all of us—is our utmost duty now. See the fear, acknowledge the fear, and then pivot.

2. **Approach reducing your fear of death as a goal-setting plan.**

This is the hardest fear to overcome, so if you can't do it immediately, don't be harsh on yourself. It takes practice and a lot of willpower to calm a worried heart. Tell a mother to not worry about her children. Tell someone in their twenties to not worry about Grandma. Of course we worry—we fear for them, for us. That's normal. But beyond that thick blanket of fear, ask yourself why you have this fear.

You can easily answer this question:

- Because you love these people dearly.
- Because the idea of not having them in your life is so devastating that it drives you crazy.
- Because you want them to stay healthy.
- Because you don't want your loved ones or you to suffer for weeks because of a severe respiratory disease.
- Because you want the very best for these people (and yourself).

These are all nice sentiments. Now that we've established the "goal" of our worry, let's see what the best we can do to achieve it is. Worry, we can agree, won't make our loved ones or us healthier, happier, or not infected. What will increase the chances of this outcome, though, are the following:

- Keeping our calm and managing our anxiety to be able to make rational decisions.

- Sharing the latest information about COVID-19 with our loved ones from reliable sources.
- Taking care of the mental health of our loved ones (and our own) by checking in, asking about how they feel, and listening nonjudgmentally.
- Making sure to follow all the safety precautions recommended by the CDC and WHO.
- Spreading words of comfort and accurate news on social media.
- Making a will. (I know, I know. This hits hard. I'm not even thirty but I'm making my will because hey, I might be in the 0.2%. While some part of me is terrified by this step, a bigger part of me feels at ease to know that whatever happens to me, my loved ones will be cared for.)
- Encourage your loved ones (and yourself) to do soul-lifting activities such as reading, meditating, watching nature

documentaries, happy movies, or trying out some artistic expression.
- Eat more healthily. Boost your immune system with nourishing food. Exercise.
- Take action. Do anything, and everything, within your power to avoid the dreaded outcomes of getting infected—or dying.

Because worry won't save neither you nor your loved ones. But taking the right actions give you a pretty good chance.

Let me tell you a secret. Even if—talking about the age group of 80+—the mortality rate is 15 percent, guess what the other 85 percent stands for? I'm not telling you this to downplay the severity of this pandemic. We don't have quite accurate numbers or data, and those who get the virus can suffer quite dearly before they get healthy—some may have permanent lung damage. So by all means, take all the safety measures death-seriously (no pun intended) to prevent pain and damage, and to avoid spreading the disease. But it's also important to realize that even if we get the virus, that doesn't mean a 100 percent chance of dying. I wish to highlight this because I know that the worried mind can broadcast such ideas.

I know that for those who have lost a loved one or are currently battling with this insidious virus, what I'm about to say will sound offensive and I'm very sorry for that, but as statistics stand today, the majority of people are about to suffer more severe consequences because of the byproducts of the virus, not the virus itself. These byproducts are the upcoming three fear categories.

Fear of Financial Loss

I could write an entire book just about this one fear. When I was eight, my family's business went bankrupt and we lost everything. When I was sixteen, my father "invested" my entire inheritance in some pyramid scheme and I lost everything. Getting to zero as a family and as an individual leaves one with a complicated relationship with money. Two years ago, I decided to invest $500 of my savings into an actual money market tool, but before I could make the transaction to fund my portfolio, I had a full-blown panic attack. Out of nowhere. All I knew was that from one moment to the next, I could hardly breathe, a huge stone was sitting on my chest, the world became blurry and my limbs were tingling, and I had to lay down in a child's pose and cry and cry. At that point in my life, investing and losing $500, luckily, wouldn't have brought me anywhere near bankruptcy. I still had a nervous breakdown.

I wanted to become better at managing money, though. I read five key books on the topic—how to invest better, how to create a sustainable financial plan that is safe enough so you can sleep well at night but risky enough to bring you margins with which you achieve your financial goals. I'm a good student, I learned the theory well.

But even now, after I have some savings, after I have financial knowledge, I'm very conflicted about investing in, say, the stock market. Everybody is telling me that this is the time to put your money in the S&P 500, the ETFs and what not. The market is tanking, a bear market is coming, so invest, invest, invest. Honestly, all I want to do is crawl under my blanket and not invest, not invest, not invest. It's hard to manage money unemotionally when you have a couple of traumatic experiences of losing everything; when you can still remember how it felt to live on pork sausage sent by your grandparents and bread for years. When your parents took you to the cheapest Chinese market to buy your essential clothes once a year. And even with that, the best you could hope for were the basics. Four-striped Adidas shoes, anyone? I remember the fear in my mom's eyes every time someone rang our bell. She was terrified it was either the gas or the electricity company to cut our access due to multiple unpaid bills. I remember those times, and my stomach still shrinks into a peanut today.

So if I tell you I can relate to how you feel if you lost a lot—or everything—in the past weeks, I mean it. When hunger and financial insecurity knocks on the door, everything else jumps out on the window: goals, aspirations, improving oneself, becoming a better person. All these new-age goals become irrelevant. I remember when well-off classmates tried to educate me on matters of a mature soul; I should look at life like this and that.

Me: "Is it money?"
Them: "No."
Me: "Can I eat it?"
Them: "No."
Me: "Then I'm not interested."

Your mind gets obsessed day and night about how to make money, pay the bills, and keep your kids fed. It's mentally and emotionally crippling. People get more snappy, impatient, even rude when they are squeezed by the wallet.

Those who are not there yet, but they have a very good chance to be, can also become overly anxious, paranoid, and emotionally volatile. It adds to the stress that one can't really know how long the current situation will last. Also, one can't really find alternative income sources. Not traditional ones, at least. There are only that many availabilities in the supermarkets and other essential stores for new laborers. There are a lot of money-making possibilities online, but the majority of people don't know how to make ends meet there.

I think it's human nature to feel that we're not making enough money. Raise your hand if you feel—or ever felt—that, yes, you make enough money, and you wouldn't be able to spend what you make even if you wanted. I'm fairly positive that not many of us would raise our hands. This is because, on one hand, indeed, we don't make that much money. On the other hand, because once we start earning more, our expenses increase proportionally. We go for the fancier wine, the tastier cheese, we shop at better brands, we get the Dior eyeliner and not the Sephora generic, and so on.

Before we notice it, boom. Our paycheck is gone. Is it not? Would you like to live in a bigger house? You know, where all your branded clothes can be neatly organized in a closet. Did you hear Tesla cars can parallel park now? Wouldn't it be nice to stop making a fool of yourself while parking? Of course it would. Bang, bang, bang. Where's the money? Right?

Shouldn't we have savings? Build an emergency fund? Sure... we should, but... Black Friday is coming up and I always wanted the Dyson hairdryer. Okay, Black Friday passed. What about now? Well, it's Christmas soon. I need money to buy presents. It's New Year's. It's my birthday. It's summer, holiday season. It's September, school time... It's Black Friday again. Christmas? Dang! It's 2020 and I didn't save a penny! Doesn't matter, this year I will! Wait, what? Coronavirus? Quarantine? Did I lose my job?

And here we are, in the present moment. We have our Tesla neatly parallel parked but we can't use it. We have the nice house and the Dyson hairdryer, but who cares? *Can I eat it?* What are we going to pay our bills with?

How many of you can relate to this story?

I'm afraid many of us. While I can't save you—who has lost everything, lost a lot, or is terrified of losing a lot—I can give you some facts, which you may find comforting. Just in the past 106 years we saw two world wars, 19 depressions or recessions in the United States alone, a major global pandemic (the Spanish flu) and some smaller ones, and we've always recovered. Always. Economies recovered. The stock market recovered. People recovered.

If you stay on the top of your game, you keep an open mind, not shy away from opportunities that fall out of your career comfort zone, and learn about budgeting, saving, and investing smartly, chances are high you'll recover, too. It might take some time, there might be periods of uncertainty and discomfort, and steps back in lifestyle. But you'll recover financially.

The key point here, just like in other fear dimensions, is to focus on what falls within your circle of influence. You can't change how governments are handling this pandemic. You can't possibly influence how the stock market is doing. You can't influence how this virus will play globally.

But you do have influence on your budgeting habits, for example. You know, there are two ways of accumulating wealth. One way is by making more money. The other way is to spend less. Take advantage of this time of quarantine and design a budgeting model that you can follow, not even in a time of scarcity, but always.

The rule of thumb of budgeting is:

- Expense allocation: 50% of your income on essentials, 30% of your income on personal needs, and 20% of your income in savings.
- Emergency fund: Have at least three months' worth of savings in your emergency fund. Keep this money liquid, easily accessible.

- Investment funds: Take advantage of 401k, IRA, and Roth IRA retirement funds and maximize them if you have the opportunity. If you have more to invest, try to open an account with a no-cost or low-cost brokerage platform like Vanguard, Robinhood, or FirstTrade, and put some money in low-cost ETFs.[2]
- Debt destruction: If you have debt, focus on paying off the one with the highest interest rate first. Ask for debt refinancing if you can.

---

[2] I am not a financial advisor. I'm just telling you what I learned from the books I read and what I'm about to do. Do your own research before you start investing in the stock market. I can recommend to you the following books to read and learn: *Get a Financial Life: Personal Finance in Your Twenties and Thirties* by Beth Kobliner and *The Bogleheads' Guide to Investing* by Taylor Larimore, Michael LeBoeuf, and Mel Lindauer.

As I told you earlier, I have my fair share of experiences when money was simply not available. But thanks to these experiences I am also certain that avoiding gathering financial intelligence is simply immature. We are adults. We need to understand how money works and how to take advantage of it; to make money serve us, not live for making money. Investing is not your thing? Fine. I can absolutely understand why. Especially if you are just getting started with having financial knowledge, diving deep into investing would be more risky.

But having and keeping a budget is absolutely necessary once you start making money. You need to know where your money comes from and where it goes. And knowledge gives you power, gives you control. I don't intend this book to be one on financial education, so I will briefly present you a very basic but effective budgeting method.

1. Figure out how much you make a year, and then break it down to a month-by-month income. Here come the tax-deducted salaries, passive income streams, inheritance, checks... Everything that is yours to spend.

2. Add together your essential expenses. Your rent, recurring utility bills, your mortgage, and other debts are considered essential. Your transportation costs can come here, too. If you know how much you usually spend on food, you can put that here, as well. These expenses can amount to 50-70% of your income—especially if you include food.

3. Put 20% of your income into your savings account. It can be easier if you automate a chunk of your salary to your savings account month by month and you don't even calculate it as income. If you can't

possibly put 20% of your salary into savings without compromising your essentials, then automate 10%. Or 5%. Anything is better than nothing. The only exception to this rule is if you have high-interest debts. In that case, group the amount of money you'd put into a savings account into paying off that debt. The quicker you pay it off, the less extra money you'll pay over time. Once your high-interest debt is gone, you can start saving.

4. If you "paid" your savings account 20% and you bought all your essentials, it's time for fun! Whatever remains (ideally 30%) in your wallet, you can spend it as you find pleasant. Would you like a new couch? A fancy dinner? A wellness weekend? Go for it! Pamper yourself. That money is for your personal happiness. Of course, if you wish to save more, you can. You don't have to spend any money just

for the sake of spending. If you'd like to have a longer vacation in the summer (assuming that we can), save the monthly extra money for that. Or for whatever you want but you can't afford buying in one go.

With financial matters, I need to be a bit draconian. I shouldn't lick your wounds if you made poor financial choices in the past. I don't do you a favor if I say, "It's okay you didn't build an emergency fund. It's okay you avoided getting a financial life up to your forties." It's not okay. You made bad decisions when you didn't prioritize these two things in your life. The current situation you're facing can shed light on it. But your life is not over. You can get out of this rut. You can start budgeting today. You can start reading the books I recommended today. You need to take action to build a financially more secure future for yourself and your family.

Fear of Losing Connection

When I was in my final year at university, I took up an acting class for extra credits. Our exam in this class was about portraying a serious problem we face today in society. There were many creative people in my class impersonating our politicians, bankers, social media "tragedies," the perpetual mother-in-law dilemma. While there were serious parts in each performance, they also generated a lot of laughter. People seemed to have some moment of recognition of the character on stage—somehow they could relate to the presented experience.

And then came a female classmate of mine. Her performance was different. She portrayed a homeless person. She came to perform in ragged and dirty clothing, surrounded herself with cardboard and bags of garbage. While muttering to herself, she walked around the class, trying to catch our eye, asking for help, money, tobacco, and having a mental breakdown when all of us, just like in real life, turned away uncomfortably. Recalling her performance still gives me chills.

There was an important message in the contrast of the presented characters during this exam. Most of the people while presenting their character alone still had a sense of connection with us, the audience. The mother-in-law, the banker, the politician all *existed* to us. The homeless woman was also alone while performing, but her persona was tangled in such a powerful existential pain that no one could—or wished—to relate with.

I wanted to tell you this story because it sheds light on a general yet rarely spoken or acknowledged fear. And this fear is greater than hunger, or struggling to stay clean, or to have a job, or a rooftop over your head. This is a fear about losing something we mostly take for granted: a connection to others that serves as protection which we all rely upon.

Some people don't like being alone. Even the thought is a fear trigger for them. Some people love being alone; that's the state where they feel inner peace. But as we discussed earlier, being alone is not the same thing as being lonely, isolated, *disconnected*.

Disconnection is a terrifying experience. Today's world is drifting to a (fingers crossed) temporary place where we are encouraged to stay away from each other physically. Some might righteously fear that they face the threat of full disconnection from society. The feeling that we could start to disappear is a chilling one. One of humanity's biggest fears is becoming someone no one is interested in being involved with or help in any way. When we're in a full lockdown, it is natural that thoughts like these pop up in our mind. Some people are not terrified of disconnection on this level, but they fear emotional distancing, a weakening of friendships and relationships.

In times like these, it is more important than ever to make a conscious effort to stay connected. On one hand, to help others—on the other hand, to help ourselves. The internet and social media, as demonized as they were in the past few years, are our only source of connection at the moment. They both are neutral vessels. We can use them to do good, or to do bad. We can use them to spread hope, support, love, and uplifting thoughts. Or we can be fearmongers, conspiracy theorists, trolls, and what not. This is a time when it is more important than ever to check on your elderly relatives, your friends who you know to be loners, and people who you haven't talked to for a long time.

A few days ago, a Facebook friend of mine texted me. I honestly didn't even remember where I knew him from. I must have added him as a friend around 2014 when it was cool to have 2000+ friends. He asked me how I was doing and if I was safe. It felt so good to receive this little note of kindness from this... well, practically-a-stranger virtual friend. Human kindness and caring. Connection. It doesn't take much to give and get them.

The antidote for the fear of losing connection is the conscious effort to maintain and initiate connections.

Here is a practice you can do. Set a daily goal, a quota, so to say, for how many people you will text. You can have two groups, a group for "fixed" people, like your children, parents, partner (if you're apart), and best friend who you reach out to daily. And then have a set number of miscellaneous people who you text only weekly, or monthly, about their wellbeing. Have at least seven conversations going each day. They don't even need to be long. You can just exchange a few sentences.

Another thing you can do is a planned and organized virtual... blank—virtual happy hour, virtual family assembly, virtual friend zone, etc. There is an amazing application I'm using, it works for Android and iOS alike, called *House Party*. This app brings all the people who join the same virtual room on one screen. So if your aunt in Colombia, your dad in Malaysia, your brother in Germany, and you in the US want to have a virtual happy hour together (although the time zone difference will need some serious planning), all you have to do is download this app, sign in to your room, and you can see everyone on the same screen. I tried this method the other day. Nine family members joined—and talked—at the same time. It was a beautiful, chaotic get-together, everyone sipping their little drinks (strictly tea) and sharing stories. It almost felt like sitting in the same room, talking. I can't recall a time when these nine family members sat in the same room before. Give this app (or any other similar app) and the experience it provides a try.

Don't forget that you can also connect with people you don't know or who are not even alive anymore. How? Through books, of course.

This is a great time to read biographies, books based on true stories, history books, everything that is related to human connection. A good, cheesy romance book is also a great choice, of course. But any book can help, really. Keep your days filled with impressive life paths, people—real or fictional—going the distance, conquering the odds. Laugh, cry, get immersed, get excited… books can elicit all these emotions.

Our body can't travel now, but out imagination can. Read about faraway countries, watch beautiful nature documentaries. Keep beauty and adventure alive in your room. Share what you read about with people close to you.

Keep a blog about your readings. Record everything you read on www.goodreads.com. I record every book I've read there since 2018. It is a great way to keep track of the books you read and to take some notes about the impressions the book made on you. I love to revisit my notes and recall what I loved about a book. I sometime even choose to re-read some books, they were so good.

Lastly, while practicing social distancing and trying to live our life the best way we can, let's:

- Not judge and hurt people for how they are reacting to the current situation. We can't control them, and getting annoyed will only harm our mental wellbeing.
- Acknowledge and feel our emotions.
- Allow ourselves to feel the discomfort the quarantine is creating.
- Try to be less busy and overwhelmed.
- Practice self-care and turn it into a daily routine.
- Practice gratitude daily and count our blessings.

- Practice patience.
- Practice healthy boundaries with our loved ones, ourselves, the news we consume.
- Do the best we can with what we have and from where we are.

Existential Crises

Broadly speaking, everything we talked about before are part of an existential crisis: fearing to lose or losing a loved one in death, facing the reality of our own death, financial vulnerability, or feeling socially unfulfilled. In this section I will talk about the anxiety, stress, and depression people may feel, and how to manage them when in an existential crisis in general.

Licensed therapist Katie Leikam defined existential crisis as follows, "People can have an existential crisis when they start to wonder what life means, and what their purpose or the purpose to life as a whole is. It can be a break in thinking patterns where you suddenly want answers to life's big questions."[xiii]

Facing an uncontrollable, global phenomenon, like this virus spreading and killing people, we inevitably gain understanding of how insignificant, how little our control over our life actually is. When we face the power of Mother Nature and all we can do is helplessly wait, it may bring up the question in us, "What was I thinking all along? What's my role here? Do I really mean something? Or the lives of those who perished in this pandemic?" Or tornado, or wildfire, or tsunami, or earthquake. Whoever has survived a natural disaster, I bet, has a different perspective on life and our actual power to influence it. Even the "common" natural disasters require us to do something, to take action: run, leave your house, help extinguish the fire, help others move, get out of the way of the tornado. We still may feel a sense of control and ownership over our lives. We have an active part in our survival chances—

dumbing it down, the faster and further we run, the safer we will be.

There's nowhere to run now. What's more, we're advised (and in some countries outright ordered under the penalty of perjury) to stay home. We are fighting an invisible enemy which has spread everywhere. Even with the best safety precautions we practice, we can't be totally safe. Even if we become the equivalent of the fastest and furthest runner, we are still running in circles, and we can't be absolutely safe. "Was this what I was born for? What's the meaning in all of this?"

"An existential crisis can affect anyone at any age, but many experience a crisis in the face of a difficult situation." [xiv] And we face so many difficulties now. Beyond what we talked about earlier—the increased risk of dying, the decreased financial stability and social closeness—there are other worries that can make us anxious.

For example, those who have children find themselves in a difficult position now. There is no school, no preschool—everything is closed, possibly until September. How will the kids get a quality education? It is already hard to take care of youngsters 24/7 indefinitely, without help, without a nanny or grandma. Who will have the mental power to educate, teach, and discipline the kid as a teacher would in school? *Me? Who's living off Ibuprofen and daydreams of Nirvana? The other parent who, for better or worse, decided that the best way to cope with the quarantine is to finally take some online cooking classes and is busy, thank you very much? Online tutors? Sure, that sounds like a good solution. But who is a good tutor? How can I know for sure?*

It's a hard call for any parent to make sound decisions for their children's education now. Of course they want the best for their kids. In case your child's school didn't take any measures to guarantee online tutoring for the kids, you don't need to stay totally helpless, either. Our physical mobility is limited right now but the online world has no boundaries. Go online, type in Google "online school covid" or similar keywords, and see what shows up. Do your research, read feedbacks and reviews, ask for credentials, ask for the possibility to reach out to other parents who use the service of the online school in question. For me, this was the first school that popped up using the keywords mentioned above: https://www.k12.com/coronavirus.html. I have not much information about them, but they have a professional website and live chat possibility—those are always good signs.

I am currently living under the same roof as my boyfriend, who has two roommates. One of them is my friend, with whom we had the Witch's Brew business idea, remember? He is 22, an engineer, and designs parts for a space shuttle. I have another good friend who currently lives in Oxford, England. He is in his fifties, an ex-musician, and I consider him as a kind of mentor. I had the same conversation with both of them. The talk revolved around the golden question, "What are you the most afraid about in these challenging times?" They gave two totally different answers:

"Things will never be the same."
"Things will go back to the same."

My ex-musician friend was who told me he's afraid things will never be the same. He explained his answer. He expressed his worry for the future as the concept of social gatherings. Now that people realize that everything can be done from home and are traumatized by the devastating prospects of the pandemic, many might choose to not attend large social event anymore. This could be the end of live music shows as we know it, cinema as we know it, large conferences as we know it. He has lots of musician friends who became jobless from one day to the next. Their livelihood depended on the restaurant or bar where they played every night. What will happen with the world of cinematography? Will we have even bigger TVs now? Will new movies be available on TV directly now instead of public cinemas? How will technology adapt to the changed needs? Will someone invent a tool with which we can watch a movie or "go" to a concert and get an even better experience than from what we're used to? How can a machine reproduce the pulsing and ecstasy of a larger crowd? Maybe we'll see.

What about offices? Why would anyone pay hefty rent, furniture, and office coffee to people who can do their job perfectly well from home, too? What's the future of small- to medium-sized, office-based businesses? What's the future of traveling? In the light of the dangers intercontinental travel can have, will prices rise so high that flying will become again the privilege of the rich? How will all those countries and industries that revolve around tourism respond?

I was listening to my friend, who is one of the smartest and most rational people I know, and a cold chill ran down my spine. He is not Nostradamus, what he's thinking about may or may not happen. But just the mere possibility of these options is mind-blowing. What did we think about any of these things, say, on Valentine's Day?

My friend also added that all the changes he fears may not necessarily prove to be bad in the long run. Businesses and professions will adapt to the new world order over time. He is hopeful that if, indeed, offices and mass social gatherings will not require people to congregate in busy city centers, we'll slowly spread out to the countryside, become more in touch with nature, be less stressed and busy and in a rush all the time, and live life with more gratitude and simplicity. There will be less pollution, less FOMO, and less anxiety. It's not a bad image.

My other friend, the engineer, said he fears things will go back to the way they were. He elaborated that he's terrified of the majority of people not learning the important lessons these times teach us; that after a week of the quarantine being lifted, we will forget how hard and miserable it was in the COVID era and readapt to life's normalcy with its goods and bads. Ever since the quarantine started, pollution drastically decreased in China, the Bay Area, and pretty much the entire globe. Here is a photo taken by NASA about the pollution change in China after the COVID-19 outbreak:

NASA's Earth Observatory pollution satellites show "significant decreases" in air pollution over China since the coronavirus outbreak began.
Courtesy of NASA.

Picture 3: China's past and current pollution rate[xv]

My engineer friend is happy for the unintended positive consequences of the pandemic. Governments and corporations are forced to decrease production, and thus pollution, now. But at the same time, the unintended emissions decline only sheds light on how poorly equipped and behind companies truly are to handle the other major world threat, global warming. Emissions should be more or less the same as they are now. But now, they're low because of the restrictions due to a catastrophe, not because corporations actually found a way to decrease emissions. Experts fear that the pollution decrease is temporary, and once the virus outbreak is tamed, it will go back to what it was before.

"The pandemic is fast, shining a spotlight on our ability or inability to respond to urgent threats. But like pandemics, climate change can be planned for in advance, if politicians pay attention to the warnings of scientists who are sounding the alarm," said Peter Gleick, a climate scientist and founder of the Pacific Institute in Berkeley, California.[xvi]

Just as a means of comparison, here is some data from experts published in Forbes. "Worldwide, air pollution kills an estimated 7 million people annually, including about 100,000 Americans. Air pollution may also affect the mortality rate of COVID-19. Early analyses have identified hypertension as the leading simultaneous chronic disease (comorbidity) in patients who have died from COVID-19. Studies have linked air pollution, particularly NO2, to hypertension."[xvii]

It's fascinating how the world went all crazy to address the threat of the coronavirus, yet about seven million people are dying yearly from pollution and no drastic action has been taken to address that killer.

Both of my friends have a point. It's both scary to think about what is going to happen if the world will never be the same or if it *will* be the same. My hope lies somewhere in between these two views. I don't think we'll change as much as my ex-musician friend predicted, but also, it won't be exactly the same as before.

The more relevant question for us to answer is, what do we want our role to be in the future, however that future may be? Who do we want to be? What values do we want to deliver? How do we want to find significance? How do we want to show up for others? What will security and insecurity mean to us? How much gratitude will we have in our life? What impact do we want to have on our environment?

Whatever is about to come will come, and we as individuals have little impact on it. So we should focus on things that fall within our circle of influence: our behavior, our values, our emotional, mental, physical wellbeing, and the support we give and receive. If everyone planted their own roses, there would be flowers in every garden. Plant your roses and enjoy them. Lead by example.

Existential crises are not necessarily bad. They force us to take a closer look at how we live, who we are, and who we want to become. Answer the questions above and start designing your future, post-pandemic self.

Chapter 5—How to De-escalate Conflict at Home

Conflict happens, even in the best relationships. If your relationship is going through a harder phase at the moment, being locked in together 24/7—or the opposite, being separated indefinitely—can take a toll on you and your partner. Learning conflict management tools, therefore, can be a valuable time investment to enhance our wellbeing and our relationships. The tools I'm about to present can be used at any time, in any phase of life; not only when the world is ending. Right now, they are more important because we have nowhere to go and no one else to hug for comfort. We can't go and have a sleepover at our best friend's while "the jerk" reconsiders their life and says sorry. While the current situation is not optimal, it is a great chance to stop avoiding problems and start addressing hurts in real time so they won't have time to fester.

When two people are in a healthy, loving relationship, they accept the other person; they love them "warts and all." After seeing the best and the worst in someone and still wanting to be together means that there is a deeper connection. Assuming that the two of you have known each other for a while, you might have already discovered what the biggest trigger point of the other person is. What is the spot on which, if you step on it, your partner gets reactive over? If you haven't discover the "magic spot" yet, it can be a good time to talk about each other's soft spots when both of you are in a calm head space. In times of isolation it is essential to find, and have compassion for, that one soft spot that the other person has; where your partner needs to be handled with gentleness, regardless of how much sense it may or may not make to you.

In every healthy relationship, you'll find this dynamic. There is that "one thing"—the Achilles heel—that each partner has, which usually is not that relatable to the other partner. Each partner needs to be allowed to have their "one thing." This is usually a pain point or a sensitivity left over from childhood, and once the other partner discovers this "weakness" in the other, the choices are:

- to be supportive and compassionate, leading to a healthy relationship; or
- to be dismissive and shaming, leading to a toxic relationship.

Think or inquire about your partner's soft spot, and also take a mental note of yours. One of you may not be bothered by snappiness and constant anxiety, but the other is. One of you may be comfortable with direct, firm words coming from others, but the other may feel shamed and criticized when spoken to that way.

Why am I emphasizing this so much? Because it's safe to say that these soft spots can become deal breakers when they are not accepted by the other. When a person has an issue that is so emotionally triggering for them, and their partner keeps poking that issue, it's a formula for a stressful relationship. But when two partners can see clearly where their partner's pain point is, and they say, "I'm okay with that," and they consciously work on not poking this emotional bruise, so to speak, then feelings of love and trust emerge. Which leads to intimacy—both emotional and physical.

My first piece of advice, thus, is that conflict de-escalation is rather conflict prevention. Be present—be mindful—of your partner's needs and your own.

Another conflict prevention measure is discussing your need for sp…ace.

Personal space is very important when it comes to restoring the alignment with one's self. Everybody needs time for themselves, even if they are together with people who they love dearly. Needing personal space looks different for each person. It is a good time to get a good, clear understanding of what "needing space" looks like for you and your partner. The challenge in this question is how to take space without abandoning the other person. The answer lies in defining what space means and communicating about it openly, and the feelings that come up around it. Some people need to have a lot of time alone to feel good in their own skin. Other people need physical and emotional closeness very often, especially in anxiety-provoking times such as these.

There's a productive way and a destructive way to get space when you're in a relationship. The productive way (adding the quarantine perk) may look like going to another room separately to spend time with a friend on the phone, engaging in separate hobbies, or watching a movie alone, for example. Being in the same room with your partner, yet tuning them out or being at a distance emotionally, can be very destructive to the partnership, from an emotional standpoint. You want to work toward the productive ways, and make sure the destructive ways are kept to a minimum when you agree on what space means to each of you. It can be challenging to find the place where neither of you feel too ignored or too overwhelmed by engagement. If your "space needs" are drastically different, you can get creative about how to solve the problem.

For example, the partner who wants more space can tell the other partner to watch a movie or read a book that means a lot to them. This way, the partner with the need of more closeness can feel close to their loved one even if they are not in the same space. You can try to alternate between one's space needs. One day one sacrifices at the altar of more closeness, the other day the other person makes sacrifices to provide enough time and space. Make sure to stay nonjudgmental and kind about the other's needs.

What can you do if, even against your best intentions to prevent conflict, you can sense tension rising? Being prepared for potential conflict is not negative or crazy thinking, it's smart. There are several verbal and nonverbal cues that foreshadow tension, and you can catch them in time if you pay attention. The following cues are usually signs of an unfolding conflict:

- Clenched fists or tightening of one's jaw.
- A sudden shift in body language.
- A change in the tone used during a conversation.
- Pacing or fidgeting.
- A change in eye contact.

- An attempt to try to look bigger: bulging chest, arms distancing from the body, straighter back.
- Signs of emotional overheating like yelling, gaslighting, defiance, regression, mocking, bullying, provocative questions, or stonewalling.

What can you do when you notice any of these signs in your partner?

Before you engage with them, make sure that you're calm. If you're tense as well, your reaction will only escalate the situation. Calm down first; take deep breaths. Ask yourself, "What am I trying to convey? What outcome am I seeking from this conversation? Is this the best time and place to have this conversation?" Maybe your partner burned their hand while preparing breakfast and they growled at you while they were in pain. Telling them they were rude while they're cooling their hand in a bucket might not be the best time.

Also, it is a good thought to pick your battles; talking about every minor issue might not be worth your energy.

If the offense was indeed severe, you're calm, and you know what your goal is with the conversation, open up the discussion with "I" statements and focus on your feelings instead of delivering your message in an accusatory tone.

For example, say, "When you burned your hand and said *XYZ* to me, I felt scared, hurt, and helpless. Can we talk about it?" instead of, "When you burned your hand and said *XYZ* to me, you made me feel scared, hurt, and helpless. You need to stop that!" It is a subtle change in phrasing, but it actually doesn't point a finger at the other person and the solution request doesn't sound so harsh.

Regardless of how you phrase things, there's still a chance the other person will not respond kindly.

If that happens, avoid getting defensive, even if their rage is directed at you. When you see the argument escalating, take a break or let it go for now. You can always come back to a topic later.

If your partner responds favorably, let them finish their point before responding. Look at your conflict as a learning opportunity, not a battle. It's you two against the problem. It is smart to establish rules in times of "peace" about how you're going to handle conflicts in the future. When one of you breaks these rules, the other can make a comment as a reminder, and at the second time the rules are violated, the other party can distance themself temporarily from the conversation.

Knowing how to argue improves your chances of communicating well. Arguments can be a healthy exchange of ideas instead of a battlefield.

If you are the one who hurt your partner in some way and they open up to you about it, here is how to manage the situation.

Listen carefully to what your partner tells you. Acknowledge their feelings without passing judgment on them. Show some empathy; even if you do not agree with your partner's position, accept that from their point of view what they say makes sense. Try to express understanding of why your partner feels a particular way; this is a big step in de-escalating the conflict. Ask for clarification if something is unclear. Paraphrase what your partner said to assure them you care. Asking open-ended questions can help reassure your partner that you care, that you have understood their frustrations, and that you are open to finding a solution to the problem. It is always good to ask for your partner's wishes and their ideas for a solution.

When you feel you helped your partner get rid of their negative emotions, you can ask if they want to hear your take on the matter. This is the time where you can explain yourself using "I" statements, take responsibility for what you did wrong, and apologize when needed. Avoid invalidating your partner's complaints while you talk about your side. Don't be quick to offer solutions unless asked otherwise.

For example, "I'm sorry I lashed out at you when I burnt my hand but you shouldn't take everything so sensitively." is hardly an apology. It is criticism and judgment in disguise. Instead, say something along the lines of, "I'm sorry I lashed out at you when I burnt my hand. I was in pain, but that's not a good reason to take it out on you. I feel bad for making you feel scared, hurt, and helpless. That was absolutely not my intention, but I can see why you felt that way. I will try to handle my frustrations better in the future." This way, you acknowledge the pain you caused, you validate your partner ("I can see why you felt that way."), and you pledge to change in the future. Now, this apology will only have a lasting positive impact on your relationship if you indeed start working on yourself and try different techniques to decrease your reactivity.

Closing a conflict with a sincere apology and a real commitment to change will leave you in a better place as a couple. If you wish to learn more about how to give an honest apology, read Gary Chapman's book *When Sorry Isn't Enough*. He talks about the five languages of apology. He says everybody understands and is open to receive apology differently, so if you want to score an A+ apology with your partner (or you want them to learn about your apology language), read this book together and discuss the solutions proposed.

This time can really bring us together or push us apart as couples. Whichever will happen is completely up to us. If we let it happen, we can get to know our partner and ourselves on a much deeper level.

In Closing…

We are facing something unprecedented in our lifetime. This can be scary, and we may feel we're alone. But we aren't. We all have each other. Your neighbor is right next to you. Your mom is thinking about you. You can appreciate more than ever before that you have someone to hug. Take refuge in the good that still surrounds you. There is always good—just allow yourself to see it.

I am here for you. I hope my words gave you a few hours of comfort. I hope you will try out some of the tips I've shared with you. I hope you and your loved ones stay safe. I hope you find your own meaning in this suffering.

Remember, it is healthy to ask for what you need in your relationships. Some people will respect and acknowledge your needs and some won't. But asking for what you need grants you the opportunity to live your best life and gives people the chance to show up for you in ways that matter to you. Asking for your needs to be met is a position of power. You don't have to be helpless. Similarly, pay attention when people express their needs to you and how they need you to show up for them. Treat their request as you would want your request to be treated. It's as simple as that.

While grounding yourself in reality, trust that this moment is teaching you something valuable. Trust that you will be okay without knowing how things are going to unfold. Trust that life is preparing you for something better. Trust in human kindness. Trust that your needs will be met. Trust that you're not alone. Trust while you're patiently waiting.

Trust in living without having all the answers.

Love,

Zoe

Before you go...

How did you like this book? Would you consider leaving a feedback about your reading experience so other readers could know about it? If you are willing to sacrifice some of your time to do so, there are several options you can do it:

1. Leave a review on Amazon.
2. Leave a review on goodreads.com. Here is a link to my profile where you find all of my books. https://www.goodreads.com/author/show/14967542.Zoe_McKey
3. Send me a private message to zoemckey@gmail.com
4. Tell your friends and family about your reading experience.

Your feedback is very valuable to me to assess if I'm on the good path providing help to you and where do I need to improve. Your feedback is also valuable to other people as they can learn about my work and perhaps give an independent author as myself a chance. I deeply appreciate any kind of feedback you take time to provide me.

Thank you so much for choosing to read my book among the many out there. If you'd like to receive an update once I have a new book, you can subscribe to my newsletter at www.zoemckey.com. You'll get My Daily Routine Makeover cheat sheet and Unbreakable Confidence checklist for FREE. You'll also get occasional book recommendations from other authors I trust and know they deliver good quality books.

Brave Enough

Time to learn how to overcome the feeling of inferiority and achieve success. Brave Enough takes you step by step through the process of understanding the nature of your fears, overcome limiting beliefs and gain confidence with the help of studies, personal stories and actionable exercises at the end of each chapter.

Say goodbye to fear of rejection and inferiority complex once and for all.

Less Mess Less Stress

Don't compromise with your happiness. "Good enough" is not the life you deserve - you deserve the best, and the good news is that you can have it. Learn the surprising truth that it's not by doing more, but less with Less Mess Less Stress.

We know that we own too much, we say yes for too many engagements, and we stick to more than we should. Physical, mental and relationship clutter are daily burdens we have to deal with. Change your mindset and live a happier life with less.

Minimalist Budget

Minimalist Budget will help you to turn your bloated expenses into a well-toned budget, spending on exactly what you need and nothing else.

This book presents solutions for two major problems in our consumer society: (1) how to downsize your cravings without having to sacrifice the fun stuff, and (2) how to whip your finances into shape and follow a personalized budget.

Rewire Your Habits

Rewire Your Habits discusses which habits one should adopt to make changes in 5 life areas: self-improvement, relationships, money management, health, and free time. The book addresses every goal-setting, habit building challenge in these areas and breaks them down with simplicity and ease.

Tame Your Emotions

Tame Your Emotions is a collection of the most common and painful emotional insecurities and their antidotes. Even the most successful people have fears and self-sabotaging habits.

But they also know how to use them to their advantage and keep their fears on a short leash. This is exactly what my book will teach you – using the tactics of experts and research-proven methods.

Emotions can't be eradicated. But they can be controlled.

The Art of Minimalism

The Art of Minimalism will present you 4 minimalist techniques, the bests from around the world, to give you a perspective on how to declutter your house, your mind, and your life in general. Learn how to let go of everything that is not important in your life and find methods that give you a peace of mind and happiness instead.

Keep balance at the edge of minimalism and consumerism.

The Critical Mind

If you want to become a critical, effective, and rational thinker instead of an irrational and snap-judging one, this book is for you. Critical thinking skills strengthen your decision making muscle, speed up your analysis and judgment, and help you spot errors easily.

The Critical Mind offers a thorough introduction to the rules and principles of critical thinking. You will find widely usable and situation-specific advice on how to critically approach your daily life, business, friendships, opinions, and even social media.

The Disciplined Mind

Where you end up in life is determined by a number of times you fall and get up, and how much pain and discomfort you can withstand along the way. The path to an extraordinary accomplishment and a life worth living is not innate talent, but focus, willpower, and disciplined action.

Maximize your brain power and keep in control of your thoughts.

In The Disciplined Mind, you will find unique lessons through which you will learn those essential steps and qualities that are needed to reach your goals easier and faster.

The Mind-Changing Habit of Journaling

Understand where your negative self-image, bad habits, and unhealthy thoughts come from.

Know yourself to change yourself. Embrace the life-changing transformation potential of journaling. This book shows you how to use the ultimate self-healing tool of journaling to find your own answers to your most pressing problems, discover your true self and lead a life of growth mindset.

Stretch Your Mind

This book collects all the tips, tricks and tactics of the most successful people to develop your inner smartness.

The Unlimited Mind will show you how to think smarter and find your inner genius. This book is a collection of research and scientific studies about better decision-making, fairer judgments, and intuition improvement. It takes a critical look at our everyday cognitive habits and points out small but serious mistakes that are easily correctable.

Who You Were Meant To Be

Discover the strengths of your personality and how to use them to make better life choices. In Who You Were Born To Be, you'll learn some of the most influential personality-related studies. Thanks to these studies you'll learn to capitalize on your strengths, and how you can you become the best version of yourself.

Wired For Confidence

Do you feel like you just aren't good enough? End this vicious thought cycle NOW. Wired For Confidence tells you the necessary steps to break out from the pits of low self-esteem, lowered expectations, and lack of assertiveness. Take the first step to creating the life you only dared to dream of.

How To Be Whole Again

In this essential book, bestselling author and former confidence coach, Zoe McKey, exposes the harmful consequences emotional unavailability and toxic relationships can have. Experiences with such people create a feeling of neglect, inadequacy, or unworthiness. Find ways to heal from the pain.

Within your environment toxic people can be found; in your family, relationship, workplace, even places of worship. Free yourself from emotionally immature people and regain your true nature.

To access the full list of my books visit this link.

Reference

Centers for Disease Control and Prevention. Know the facts about coronavirus disease 2019. CDC. 2020. https://www.cdc.gov/coronavirus/2019-ncov/symptoms-testing/share-facts.html

Hahn, Thich Nhat. Overcoming the Fear of Death. Dharma Talk Plum Village. 1997. https://www.dhammatalks.net/Books2/Thich_Nhat_Hanh_Overcoming_the_Fear_of_Death.htm

Higuera, Valencia. What Is an Existential Crisis, and How Do I Break Through It? Healthline. 2018. https://www.healthline.com/health/existential-crisis#what-is-it

McMahon, Jeff. New Satellite Video Shows China Pollution Vanishing During COVID-19 Lockdown—Then Coming Back. Forbes. 2020. https://www.forbes.com/sites/jeffmcmahon/2020/03/22/video-watch-from-space-as-air-pollution-vanishes-over-china-during-coronavirus-lockdown-then-returns/#586ea87135f0

Newburger, Emma. Air pollution falls as coronavirus slows travel, but scientists warn of longer-term threat to climate change progress. CNBC. 2020. https://www.cnbc.com/2020/03/21/air-pollution-falls-as-coronavirus-slows-travel-but-it-forms-a-new-threat.html

Norem, Julie K. The Positive Power of Negative Thinking. Basic Books. 2002.

SAMHSA. Taking Care of Your Behavioral Health: Tips for Social Distancing, Quarantine, and Isolation During an Infectious Disease

Outbreak. SAMHSA. 2020 https://store.samhsa.gov/product/Taking-Care-of-Your-Behavioral-Health-Tips-for-Social-Distancing-Quarantine-and-Isolation-During-an-Infectious-Disease-Outbreak-Spanish-Version-/SMA14-4894SPANISH?referer=from_search_result

Team Tony. Do You Need To Feel Significant? Team Tony. 2020. https://www.tonyrobbins.com/mind-meaning/do-you-need-to-feel-significant/

Worldometer. Age, Sex, Existing Conditions of COVID-19 Cases and Deaths. Worldometer. 2020. https://www.worldometers.info/coronavirus/coronavirus-age-sex-demographics/

Worldometers. Coronavirus cases. Worldometers. 2020. https://www.worldometers.info/coronavirus/coronavirus-cases/

Endnotes

[i] Centers for Disease Control and Prevention. Know the facts about coronavirus disease 2019. CDC. 2020.
https://www.cdc.gov/coronavirus/2019-ncov/symptoms-testing/share-facts.html
[ii] Centers for Disease Control and Prevention. Know the facts about coronavirus disease 2019. CDC. 2020.
https://www.cdc.gov/coronavirus/2019-ncov/symptoms-testing/share-facts.html
[iii] Centers for Disease Control and Prevention. Know the facts about coronavirus disease 2019. CDC. 2020.
https://www.cdc.gov/coronavirus/2019-ncov/symptoms-testing/share-facts.html
[iv] SAMHSA. Taking Care of Your Behavioral Health: Tips for Social Distancing, Quarantine, and Isolation During an Infectious Disease Outbreak. SAMHSA. 2020
https://store.samhsa.gov/product/Taking-Care-of-Your-Behavioral-Health-Tips-for-Social-Distancing-Quarantine-and-Isolation-During-an-Infectious-Disease-Outbreak-

Spanish-Version-/SMA14-4894SPANISH?referer=from_search_result
[v] Worldometers. Coronavirus cases. Worldometers. 2020.
https://www.worldometers.info/coronavirus/coronavirus-cases/
[vi] Worldometer. Age, Sex, Existing Conditions of COVID-19 Cases and Deaths. Worldometer. 2020.
https://www.worldometers.info/coronavirus/coronavirus-age-sex-demographics/
[vii] Worldometer. Age, Sex, Existing Conditions of COVID-19 Cases and Deaths. Worldometer. 2020.
https://www.worldometers.info/coronavirus/coronavirus-age-sex-demographics/
[viii] Worldometer. Age, Sex, Existing Conditions of COVID-19 Cases and Deaths. Worldometer. 2020.
https://www.worldometers.info/coronavirus/coronavirus-age-sex-demographics/
[ix] Team Tony. Do You Need To Feel Significant? Team Tony. 2020.
https://www.tonyrobbins.com/mind-meaning/do-you-need-to-feel-significant/
[x] Norem, Julie K. The Positive Power of Negative Thinking. Basic Books. 2002.
[xi] Hahn, Thich Nhat. Overcoming the Fear of Death. Dharma Talk Plum Village. 1997.
https://www.dhammatalks.net/Books2/Thich_Nhat_Hanh_Overcoming_the_Fear_of_Death.htm

[xii] Hahn, Thich Nhat. Overcoming the Fear of Death. Dharma Talk Plum Village. 1997. https://www.dhammatalks.net/Books2/Thich_Nhat_Hanh_Overcoming_the_Fear_of_Death.htm
[xiii] Higuera, Valencia. What Is an Existential Crisis, and How Do I Break Through It? Healthline. 2018. https://www.healthline.com/health/existential-crisis#what-is-it
[xiv] Higuera, Valencia. What Is an Existential Crisis, and How Do I Break Through It? Healthline. 2018. https://www.healthline.com/health/existential-crisis#what-is-it
[xv] Newburger, Emma. Air pollution falls as coronavirus slows travel, but scientists warn of longer-term threat to climate change progress. CNBC. 2020. https://www.cnbc.com/2020/03/21/air-pollution-falls-as-coronavirus-slows-travel-but-it-forms-a-new-threat.html
[xvi] Newburger, Emma. Air pollution falls as coronavirus slows travel, but scientists warn of longer-term threat to climate change progress. CNBC. 2020. https://www.cnbc.com/2020/03/21/air-pollution-falls-as-coronavirus-slows-travel-but-it-forms-a-new-threat.html
[xvii] McMahon, Jeff. New Satellite Video Shows China Pollution Vanishing During COVID-19 Lockdown—Then Coming Back. Forbes. 2020.

https://www.forbes.com/sites/jeffmcmahon/2020/03/22/video-watch-from-space-as-air-pollution-vanishes-over-china-during-coronavirus-lockdown-then-returns/#586ea87135f0